THE CRYPTO INTRO 2022

THE BASICS OF CRYPTOCURRENCY

Contents

Introduction

Crypto is red-hot right now.

Media outlets are giving crypto unprecedented airtime while the general public has been captivated by the staggering price rises seen across the board. When measured in US dollar terms, Bitcoin ballooned by over 10 times in the 2017 calendar year alone.

Beyond the tremendous increases in value, crypto has received so much attention because of the challenging questions it raises about money and the role of central authorities such as banks and governments - roles which were taken for granted in the past.

Before the start of the crypto revolution, government-issued banknotes and coins seemed to be the only conceivable forms of money. We had never known any other way in our lifetime, nor in that of our parents.

Fast-forward to today, and many members of the crypto community ardently believe that crypto is destined to replace government-issued money, just as the personal computer replaced the typewriter. If this vision is even half-right, the implications are hard to overstate. At the very least, crypto promises to substantially weaken the monopoly power of centralized institutions.

But these are still early days for crypto. And most members of the public find crypto to be, well, cryptic. As United States Senator Thomas Carper said: "Virtual currencies, perhaps most notably Bitcoin, have captured the imagination of some, struck fear among others, and confused the heck out of the rest of us."[1] Perhaps some readers can relate to that sentiment.

Truthfully, few people have an accurate understanding of how crypto works, and many are highly skeptical. *The Crypto Intro* has been written to explain everything and respond to the tough crypto questions.

But we may be getting ahead of ourselves. Before taking a look at how crypto functions, let's make sure we understand what we're talking about.

What Is Crypto?

Crypto refers to digital assets secured by **cryptography.** Cryptography is a branch of computer science which deals with privacy and encoding. Within the category of crypto, there are many different **tokens**. These tokens are the individual assets which make up the space; Bitcoin is one of these individual assets, Ethereum is another, and Litecoin is yet another.

Crypto is entirely digital - as in, it exists only as computer code. It is possible to withdraw a $20 bill from a bank account and hold it, but that is not possible with crypto. Skeptics have expressed their reservations about an asset they can't touch. To these critics, it all seems a bit too much like make-believe.

This concern over whether or not crypto is "real" must be tackled head-on. It may help to ask: is something "fake" just because it only exists in the digital realm? We send and receive digital messages through SMS, email, and instant messaging all the time, and they are real enough. These digital messages work for their intended purpose - therefore, they are real.

Crypto has the same idea at its core. And just as email has an edge over the postal service, crypto enjoys certain advantages over government-issued money, as the next chapter will explain.

Besides, it would be surprising if any readers of this book don't <u>already</u> use digital assets. Chances are strong that when you bought your copy of <u>The Crypto Intro</u>, you entered your payment details via the Internet, probably using a credit card. If that was the case, you never handed over physical cash. Operating without "tangible" banknotes or coins is already familiar to anyone who gets their earnings deposited electronically, uses direct debits to pay their utility bills, or shops online.

Therefore, using crypto as an alternative form of value transfer isn't such a huge leap from the status quo. In fact, in some cases, using crypto feels a lot like using online banking. What distinguishes crypto is more about what happens in the background. It's like the way gas-powered cars and electric cars feature a similar driving experience, and it's only upon closer inspection that it becomes clear the engines run differently.

<u>The Crypto Intro</u> aims to show readers the crypto engine and explain how it works. That way, you can have more confidence when you come to use it.

The fact that crypto is "nothing more than computer code" is absolutely no reason to dismiss it. Equally, government-issued money is "nothing more" than pieces of paper, plastic, and non-precious metals - or more commonly these days, the numbers on a screen, representing the balance recorded within a bank's database.

What gives value to crypto is the same thing that gives value to government-issued money - the trust that people have in it. Whether they realize it or not, people who trust the US dollar are actually trusting the US government not to debase their currency. But as we will see, there are strong reasons why it is not wise to place too much trust in a system where value can be controlled and manipulated by powerful central institutions.

Crypto is not government-issued, nor is it stored in banks. Instead, crypto is decentralized, which means it is not controlled by any single authority. This is critical. Computer code governs everything, including the amount in circulation. This feature renders it immune from interference. The decentralization at the heart of crypto has a clear parallel with the Internet, and throughout this book, the Internet will serve as a useful point of familiarity.

Like the Internet, crypto exists as a borderless, networked system of connected computers. The Internet is not a singular place, nor is crypto. This makes the Internet and crypto practically impossible to shut down or outlaw. No one, no matter how powerful, can point to a certain building where crypto resides, march in, and turn it off. Groups who feel threatened by crypto will certainly try - just as monopolies and cartels have always done when they feel their power slipping away - but there are insurmountable difficulties confronting those who want crypto to go away.

Crypto can transfer value in the same way the Internet enables us to transfer information; instantly, at minimal cost, without the need for third-party approval, and without censorship. As we know, the Internet has turned out to be quite a big deal - there are few aspects of life it hasn't touched. Entire industries have been killed off, and new ones have risen to take their place.

The Internet has been particularly bad news for **middlemen** (travel agents), **gatekeepers** (traditional book publishers), and those who failed to adapt (video stores). On the other hand, the Internet has also removed huge layers of cost, enabled us to communicate far more efficiently, and given free or near-free universal access to the world's information. Few would wish to go back to the old way - and regardless, there is no way to do so. Technology cannot be put back in a box.

Could crypto have similar world-changing effects? Its promise is incredible - to disrupt the antiquated financial services industry and the outlandish fees they charge. And bringing disruption to the financial sector may be just the tip of the iceberg.

A lot of smart people are betting on crypto: from Silicon Valley, to Wall Street, to legions of computer coders, to (most importantly) the early adopters using crypto every day. Perhaps after reading *The Crypto Intro*, you will join them.

Who Is This Book For?

Despite crypto appearing all over the news, most of the coverage fixates on the day-to-day price movements rather than the more detailed picture of what crypto is. It is impossible to get into the nitty-gritty of a complex subject like crypto in a two-minute segment wedged between the sports news and the weather. To do justice to crypto requires going into far greater depth.

There are other crypto books, but they are mainly accounts of the history and potential impact of crypto, or highly technical treatises written for computer programmers. The literature was clearly missing a high-quality practical guide with all the information necessary to get started.

This book has three main goals:

1. Explain the need for crypto, along with the problems inherent with the current system of centralized institutions such as government-issued currency and financial middlemen.

2. Demystify the terminology surrounding crypto. You will become confident with terms like "wallet", "mining", and "ICO".

3. Show you how to try crypto for yourself. We will cover practical steps like how to register on an exchange, how to buy crypto for the first time, and how to keep crypto secure.

The Crypto Intro is meant to be accessible to nontechnical readers. It will use lots of analogies (even if slightly imperfect) rather than resort to the more precise but less legible computer code. Readers whose eyes glaze over when they hear terms like "elliptical curve digital signature algorithm" and "distributed timestamp server" needn't worry about being blinded by jargon.

Although this book won't go into overly onerous detail, it also won't shy away from taking the time to explain important concepts. Albert Einstein once said that everything should be made as simple as possible, but no simpler. *The Crypto Intro* tries to tread the fine line between making crypto easily understood, but without oversimplifying. I have assumed a reader with no prior knowledge but also one who is ready to roll up their sleeves and get into the inner workings of crypto - including the tricky bits.

No, It Is Not Too Late To Get Started

A common lament is that the best opportunities in crypto have already passed. In its short life, Bitcoin (the first ever crypto) has gone from being valued at well under US$1 per unit to many thousands of dollars. It is assumed that such increases could never reoccur. But there is far more to crypto than Bitcoin.

Crypto is less than 10 years old as of the time of writing. If we looked at the Internet in, say, 1996, some of the largest companies that dominate today's web landscape had barely taken their first steps. Amazon was an inconsequential online store that only sold books. Google was nothing more than an academic research project by students at Stanford. The founder of Facebook hadn't even reached his teenage years. If crypto follows a similar development path as the Internet did, then there are still plenty of fortunes yet to be made. Was it "too late" to get started on the Internet in 1996? Absolutely not.

Only a tiny fraction of those who are even aware of crypto have taken the necessary steps to experience it firsthand. By reading this book and investing even a small amount, you still have the opportunity to get ahead of the vast majority.

Additionally, anyone who begins with crypto now has avoided a lot of the problems that dogged it in the earliest days. The largest online crypto exchanges of today are (for the most part) well-funded, highly professional outfits with real expertise in making this new technology secure and user-friendly. Further, all these exchanges must compete with one another to provide the best service. The initial teething issues have provided lessons which have made crypto stronger. There are still dangers to watch out for, of course - and this book will try to point these out - but it is not too late to get started with crypto. Now might just be the very best time to begin.

Notes On Names

The Crypto Intro is a book which deals with "cryptocurrency"… or "cryptoassets"… or "crypto tokens" - depending on who is asked. The names that people prefer vary, but all of them start with the same prefix: "crypto". Therefore, this book uses the abbreviated "crypto" throughout.

It is true that **cryptocurrency** is the most commonly used term for blockchain-based digital assets. But "cryptocurrency" has also become a misnomer, responsible for a great deal of confusion. I want to make it clear right from the outset: not all forms of crypto are designed to act as currency.

The word "cryptocurrency" has stuck in the public consciousness thanks to Bitcoin. Bitcoin was the first crypto. Its original mission was to use cryptography to implement a fully peer-to-peer electronic payment system - or in other words, Bitcoin was born to fill the need for a decentralized **digital currency**. It wasn't long before people merged "cryptography" together with "currency" to form the catchy-sounding "cryptocurrency".

Since then, hundreds of additional crypto tokens have arrived on the scene, many of which have very different uses. So why does the word "cryptocurrency" endure, even though a lot of these digital assets are not built to act as currencies at all?

The answer is mainly due to the following erroneous leap in logic:
- People know that US dollars, euros, and other government-issued currencies all essentially operate the same way.
- They also understand that Bitcoin is an alternative to these government-issued currencies.
- But then they mistakenly assume that all crypto tokens are pursuing the same mission as Bitcoin… just as all government-issued currencies function in the same basic way.

As a result, "cryptocurrency" is frequently - and incorrectly - used to refer to the technology as a whole. The term "cryptocurrency" still has a meaning, albeit a narrower one. Think of it this way: all ducks are birds, but not all birds are ducks. In the same way, all cryptocurrencies are cryptos, but not all cryptos are cryptocurrencies.

With all that said, an understanding of anything new is best built in stages. If a time traveler arrived from the year 1950, and you were tasked with explaining the Internet to them, it wouldn't be a good idea to try and explain everything all at once. You might start by explaining email. It would be relatively straightforward for our visitor from 1950 to come to grips with the usefulness of electronic letters which they could send instantly to anyone in the world for free. You could call a personal computer a "mailbox that works like a radio" to build their initial conception of the device (even though not strictly true). Later, once the time traveler had got the hang of email, you could slowly introduce all the other things the Internet could do, like videos, online shopping, and social media.

The Crypto Intro takes a similar approach. We will begin with Bitcoin because the problems inherent in centrally controlled money are the plainest to see. Once that groundwork has been laid, you will be better equipped to extend your understanding. Just keep in mind while reading that there is more to crypto than alternative currency.

How To Use This Book

First, *The Crypto Intro* explains why crypto matters and how it works. The next part walks you through how to get your first crypto and how to start using it. The final chapters cover more advanced topics, including perspectives on the controversial issues surrounding crypto.

Everything in bold typeface is described in the glossary at the back of the book. This offers you a single reference place to remind yourself what the key terms mean.

You will find all the critical crypto concepts right here inside this book. But when it comes to specific websites to visit and tools to use, *The Crypto Intro* often refers to online resources, so that the information in this book will not quickly go out of date. The crypto ecosystem is subject to constant change - various services open, close, and merge. Therefore, readers should refer to the online resources linked throughout to get the most up-to-date information.

Finally, realize this: you will get the most out of *The Crypto Intro* if you take action and sign up to an exchange, get a crypto wallet, put a little money into it, use that money to buy your first crypto, and try using it to make a payment. By taking these steps, readers will master the subject material far more easily.

If you decide to participate, you should begin with a modest sum – large enough to take an interest in what happens, but small enough that it will not ruin you if something goes wrong. Build confidence before investing too much. Depending on personal financial circumstances, you could consider starting with US$100 as a base amount.

Be Responsible

For the record - _The Crypto Intro_ is not responsible for what you choose to do with the information contained herein, nor is it advising to take a certain course of action. You should make sure to:

- Question everything.
- Form your own opinions.
- Never risk more than you can afford to lose.

There is also a full legal disclaimer notice at the back of the book.

With that out of the way, let us commence the journey. We will start by going deeper into the problems that Bitcoin solves. This will help with understanding why crypto matters and serve as motivation to learn everything else that follows.

The Case For Crypto

On the 3rd of January 2009, Bitcoin went live for the very first time. There was no fanfare - in fact, only a rather obscure cryptography group was informed about it. The news of Bitcoin's arrival was announced there by a relative newcomer calling himself "Satoshi Nakamoto". Outside the group, no one else noticed.

Bitcoin was not the first attempt to create an Internet-based form of value transfer. Others such as Hashcash, Bit Gold, and B-Money were all tried in the 1990's and early 2000's. Many of the programmers behind these early efforts were part of a collective of hacker-activists known as the "cypherpunks" - a group which included Julian Assange (of WikiLeaks fame). The cypherpunks devoted themselves and their considerable programming know-how to devise ingenious ways of protecting their privacy from what they saw as overbearing central institutions.

One of the dreams of the cypherpunks was to create a non-government system of money which eschewed the need for any sort of **trusted third party**. Trade fundamentally needs <u>two</u> parties - a buyer and a seller - but in many cases, others enter into the frame. The clearest example of a trusted third party, known to all, is a bank. Banks help buyers get paid by sellers - for a fee, of course.

Today, banks have inserted themselves into more transactions than ever, thanks to the surging demand for global connectivity. When commerce shifts to online and digital, electronic payment is needed to make it work. It is highly impractical for buyers and sellers to use physical instruments such as cash or gold to transact when they are located in disparate parts of the world.

While cash can be used to buy a cup of coffee from a local café, paying for website hosting, ordering clothing online, or setting up a recurring monthly magazine subscription is much more problematic without invoking some form of digital payment. Those sorts of services are where trusted third parties like banks have seized their opportunity.

Many people are increasingly using bank cards instead of cash even for the "coffee" type of purchases - swiping a card linked to their bank balance is more convenient than carrying cash around in their pocket. All this means that financial middlemen are more prevalent than ever.

But why is this state of affairs a problem? When we are paid by others, we receive dollars / euros / etc. into a bank account. We then use them to purchase goods and services. Government-issued money and the banking system appear to adequately fulfill our needs for payments and wealth storage - at least, on the surface.

Coming to grips with why the crypto community thinks it is worth expending so much effort on trying to loosen the grip of trusted third parties is essential to understanding why crypto matters. This chapter explains the shortcomings of the status quo. It will help you to understand what motivated the cypherpunks to try to create an alternative, what motivated Satoshi Nakamoto to finally succeed at this task with Bitcoin, and what continues to motivate crypto users to this very day.

An Island Using Stone Money

Let us take a trip to an imaginary island in a state of early civilization. The inhabitants use giant stones for money, which are up to 12 feet wide and weigh several tons. Though unwieldy, these stones have served as money on the island for generations.[2]

Such enormous stones are far too heavy to carry around. It is impractical for a buyer to pass a massive stone to a seller in the manner modern people might hand over a pocketful of coins in the present day. So, the villagers just keep track of whom the stones belong to. For example, if a villager wanted to buy their neighbor's fishing boat, they would just let the rest of the village know that one of the stones that they owned now belongs to the neighbor whom they bought the boat from.

When the village was small, this system worked fine. Everyone in the tight-knit community knew everyone else, and no one would try to cheat the system. Trust was formed through interpersonal and family ties. But lately, things haven't been going smoothly. The population has swollen to thousands, and it has become increasingly difficult to keep track of the stone-ownership system through the collective consciousness alone.

Worse, there have been instances of unscrupulous villagers taking advantage of the confusion by saying they own stones that they don't have proper claim to. They then buy goods they shouldn't rightly be able to afford and leave the seller out of pocket. The deterioration in trust has caused commerce to slow to a crawl. The villagers all agree that something must be done.

The chief of the village has an idea. He proposes to create a common, central ledger of stone ownership through a specially-appointed banker. The banker's job will be to keep track of all the villagers and maintain a record of how many stones each villager owns. No more arguments - the banker will control the one, official record.

Any villager who wants to make a payment under the new system must go to the banker and tell him about the stone transfer. The banker will then check his ledger to make sure that the villager making the payment has enough stones to their name, and if all checks out, the banker will update the record to reflect the transfer of stones from buyer to seller.

The banker isn't performing this service for free. He would collect a fee every time a transaction took place, but it seems worth it to the villagers. Thanks to the banker, the villagers no longer have to trust the strangers they were doing business with - they just have to trust the banker's records.

Everyone could again transact with confidence, and things seem to be going well. But after a while, the villagers notice new problems. The banker moves into a huge house and starts wearing fancy clothes - evidently, he is growing very rich from all those transaction fees.

In addition to his newfound wealth, the banker has also grown extremely powerful. The banker could deny an account to anyone, for any reason he liked, including to any villager the banker didn't think he could make a profit from. Life becomes hopelessly difficult for those who couldn't get a bank account because so much of the island's economic activity requires one. Any villager outside of the banking system is effectively unable to trade.

The villagers begin to grumble. The banker isn't fishing for food, teaching the young, or curing the sick. He is merely keeping track of the number of stones everyone owned, yet his occupation is the most lucrative and influential of any on the island.

Furthermore, the banker has struck up a close friendship with the village chief. The chief protects the banker's privileged position - becoming a banker requires a license, which the chief himself would grant. This serves to shield the banker from competition.

In return, the banker does as he is told by the chief. Anytime the chief commands it, the banker could tell the chief what everyone is spending their stones on. Any villager who does anything the chief disapproves of (such as funding the chief's rivals) could be in for a tough time. Offending villagers might find their accounts frozen or seized.

The villagers come to realize that by handing so much control to the banker, the stones in their name are not really theirs anymore - rather, they have fallen under the influence of the banker and the chief. Although the villagers could now have more trust in each other, they still have to trust that the banker would not unjustly enrich himself or go beyond the purview of pure record-keeping. But the high fees, the loss of privacy, and the lack of universal access suggest otherwise.

* * *

Perhaps you were hoping that the story would continue to some kind of happy ending. Unfortunately, these villagers simply didn't have the technology capable of replacing the need for a banker. Neither did anyone else - right up until the 3rd of January 2009 when Bitcoin arrived.

The same sorry state of affairs that the island villagers found themselves trapped in is not too dissimilar from today's financial system. You may already have noticed a few parallels with the plight of the villagers and the problems with the modern-day status quo. Let us look at these problems in greater detail.

Six Problems With The Status Quo

It is worth contemplating that no one would use crypto if there weren't flaws with the current financial system. Understanding these will demonstrate why the need for crypto exists.

1. Expensive Middlemen

Every time a bank intermediates a transaction, they take a cut. The glistening skyscrapers prominently situated in the world's downtown districts are often adorned with the logos of major banks and financial institutions. How can they afford such pricey real estate? Simple - through the fees which all of us are paying, all the time, often without even realizing it.

Credit cards impose a fee of a few percentage points on every transaction, charged by the banks and payment processors that facilitate them. These fees appear invisible to consumers because they are paid by the merchant.

The merchant usually absorbs the transaction fees as a cost of doing business, but when a buyer uses a credit card to pay $3.00 for a cup of coffee, the café isn't receiving $3.00. Perhaps $2.90 goes to the café, while 10 cents is retained by the various financial middlemen that facilitate the entire payment infrastructure that pulls the money from the buyer's card and deposits it into the café's account.

Consumers still end up fronting the charge through higher prices. The transaction fees incurred by the café contribute to the reason why the coffee costs $3.00 in the first place. If the middlemen weren't taking their cut from every coffee sold, then the café's costs would be lower. The going rate for a coffee would be closer to $2.90 if transaction fees weren't a reality. Alternatively, the café would be more profitable if it got to keep the full $3.00. Either way, more value would stay with the producers and consumers, rather than ending up in the hands of the financial middlemen.

A few percent may not seem like a lot, but these fees add up quickly thanks to the velocity at which money changes hands. Once receiving their $2.90, the owner of the café might go out to spend it on the milk they need to make foamy lattes - again, using a bank card. The $2.90 becomes $2.81 (the financial middlemen now having pocketed $0.19 of the original $3.00). In turn, the milk seller might use their own bank card to buy office supplies - and on it goes. Every time another transaction takes place, another few percent are sliced off.

International money payments are even more costly - try using a bank to send a payment from one country to another, and the sender will be hit with a wire fee and a bad exchange rate, and the recipient might be charged a fee too, just to receive it.

This is a familiar problem for migrants who have families whom they want to send money home to. In a 2014 TED talk, Dilip Ratha explained that there are 180 million migrants who send money home regularly, adding up to a collective US$413 billion.[3] These migrants, who often come from impoverished countries, risk everything to find work in places where the wages are higher, so they can send money back to provide for their families at home.

To make the transfers, they need to use the likes of Western Union. Services like this can charge around 10% of the amount sent in transfer fees. These poor migrants and their families are exactly the kind of people who can least afford to lose any of the little money they do have - but until Bitcoin arrived, there wasn't much of an alternative to send digital value internationally.

2. Unsound and Debt-Based

Government-issued money works great… until it doesn't. And when it falls down, it happens very quickly. In 2015, indebted Greek banks limited depositors from withdrawing more than 60 euros per day. Queues of people, fearful that they could not get their money out, lined up at ATMs across the country. It was a timely reminder that a loss of confidence in the banking system can happen anywhere, even in the Western world. Greece is a full member of the European Union and the Eurozone - not to mention the cradle of Western civilization!

Greece is far from an isolated case. There have been countless historical instances of government-issued money losing its value due to indebtedness. Germany, Russia, Argentina, and Iceland are just a few places that have suffered huge currency devaluations over the last 100 years.

If the central government gets into too much debt, people lose faith in the currency. Then, backed into a corner, governments respond by printing money - an act which drastically devalues everyone's existing savings. Just ask a resident of Zimbabwe what happened to their savings over the last few decades thanks to government-backed hyperinflation. There are stories of people trying to use a wheelbarrow full of banknotes to buy groceries - and the shopkeeper refusing the worthless paper and demanding to keep the wheelbarrow as payment instead.

If you are concerned that crypto isn't backed by anything "tangible", then you should also level the same concern at fiat money. In 1971, Richard Nixon took the US dollar off the gold standard, meaning US dollars could no longer be converted into the equivalent quantity of gold. Since then, the only thing that backs the US dollar is "the full faith and credit" of the US government. With the US federal government currently many trillions of dollars in debt, a claim like "full faith and credit" must be called into question. Government-issued money has the millstone of debt around its neck - but crypto is completely debt-free.

Satoshi Nakamoto's original Bitcoin white paper put it best: "The root problem with conventional currency is all the trust that's required to make it work. The central bank must be trusted not to debase the currency, but the history of fiat currencies is full of breaches of that trust. Banks must be trusted to hold our money and transfer it electronically, but they lend it out in waves of credit bubbles with barely a fraction in reserve."[4]

Anytime a central authority can control the supply of money, they can manipulate it. By contrast, nobody is "in charge" of crypto in the same way that governments and central banks can dictate the supply of their currency. No central authority can arbitrarily decide to devalue crypto, representing a huge advantage over government-issued money.

3. Lack Of Privacy

Privacy is the foundation of a free society. Even those who aren't doing anything illegal or immoral may not want their activities recorded, but a great deal of our lives can be traced with scary accuracy through the bank's record of our digital payments. These records show where the account holder was, at what time, and what they bought. All fully traceable.

Physical cash also offers strong privacy, but governments are now conducting a "war on cash". Large-denomination cash banknotes are in the firing line - all so that more of our lives can be monitored by "the powers that be". As the revelations brought to light by Edward Snowden and others have shown, mass government surveillance is real and extensive.[5]

Anyone who doesn't want the government or for-profit banks to track what they are spending their money on will welcome the advent of crypto.

4. Subject To Restriction

Bank accounts can be frozen if law enforcement decides that the account holder is doing something questionable. This is usually justified in the name of preventing crime, but there are many shades of gray when it comes to what the government approves of and doesn't approve of. What about the purchase of recreational cannabis? Should they have the right to freeze a bank account in such a morally ambiguous case?

The case of WikiLeaks is illustrative. WikiLeaks is an international nonprofit organization that publishes secret information and classified media, fulfilling the role of a whistleblower. In 2010, banks, credit card companies, and PayPal froze the accounts of WikiLeaks at the request of the US State

Department.[6] Whether or not you agree with the mission of WikiLeaks, you can surely see that the ability of central authorities to shut down banking access represents a major problem from WikiLeaks' perspective.

Members of the crypto community stridently believe they should be able to do whatever they want to do with their own money. If a person cannot spend their money however they please, then it is not really their money. Under bank and government supervision, grown adults become like children who have to ask their parents for permission whether they are "allowed" to spend their savings on what they want, and are always at risk of being told "no".

5. Slow To Send & Receive

Think how slow sending a letter by post seems to us now that we have email - yet a several-day wait is <u>still</u> the speed of international bank wires. In an age where we can send video, audio, and other large files across the world in the blink of an eye, it is rather unbelievable that we still have to wait a week or more for an international payment to clear. Email made global communication instant and free, and crypto promises to do the same for value transfer.

Crypto is not quite instantaneous, but the time it takes to send and receive is measured in minutes and seconds, rather than days. When money can be sent at the speed of an email, all kinds of interesting possibilities open up. Global commerce can take place much faster.

6. Lack Of Universal Access

Adults without their own bank accounts are known as the "unbanked". The World Bank's Global Findex Database of 2017 estimated 1.7 billion people remain without a bank account - a figure which represents over 20% of humanity.[7]

In today's economy, having a bank account is critical to gain meaningful employment, start and operate a business, invest, pay for consumer items, and have access to credit. Once a person has food, clean drinking water, and shelter, access to banking may be the next most essential thing for an individual's prospects for success.

Despite how essential access to banking is, the requirements imposed by the banks themselves make acquiring an account all but impossible for many of the 1.7 billion unbanked. Banks often require proof of address - but what if someone lives in the slums and has no address? Banks often require proof of identity - but what if they don't have a driver's license or passport? What if the bank simply doesn't want to deal with them because they have too little money for the bank to earn a profit on? It all adds up to keeping the disadvantaged trapped in their place.

The situation is actually even worse than it first appears. People who have bank accounts can still suffer from suboptimal access. Those who have the misfortune to come from a country with a weak banking reputation - say, Nigeria - will have the usefulness of their bank account severely curtailed. People instinctively recoil when asked to send a payment to a Nigerian bank account - there's too much negative stigma attached. As a result, plenty of perfectly honest Nigerians suffer from banking discrimination, based on the unhappy accident of where they happened to be born. Crypto completely removes this problem - the crypto of a Nigerian is treated identically to the crypto of an American.

* * *

The pre-Bitcoin cypherpunks intuited that the advent of the Internet might finally facilitate a solution to the drawbacks of the existing money system. But although these brilliant programmers were able to develop clever ways to cut governments and banks out of the equation, coming up with a system which didn't replace them with another trusted third party proved a real stumbling block.

Invariably, all of their solutions required some kind of central authority to regulate functions such as how much currency to issue and counterfeit prevention. But, given the goal was to remove trusted third parties of all kinds (not merely replace them with different ones), these solutions were incomplete.

It took Satoshi Nakamoto to bring it all together with Bitcoin - the breakthrough which marked the beginning of crypto as we know it. Bitcoin was the first to totally remove trusted third parties from the architecture of the network. We will see how in the next chapter.

Though it seems unbelievable, almost nothing is known of Satoshi Nakamoto. We don't even know whether "Satoshi Nakamoto" is a real name, or even whether the name represents a single person or a group working collaboratively. Nakamoto has never appeared in public, and all we have to go on are his (her? their?) forum posts and emails, none of which carry any identifying information.

Vigorous attempts have been made to track Nakamoto down - all of which have failed. As a skilled cryptography expert, Nakamoto has proved highly adept at covering his tracks.

The mystery surrounding Satoshi Nakamoto has been an enduring fascination for the crypto community, but let us quickly move on - that story has already been told elsewhere and is not the focus of this book. Though people will continue to wonder about the identity of the inventor, the invention matters far more. Let's now turn our attention to how Bitcoin works.

How Bitcoin Works

This chapter explains how Bitcoin presents an alternative to the government-issued money system. But before delving into Bitcoin and blockchain technology, it pays to ask something even more basic.

What Is Money?

Money is a human invention for fulfilling specific needs: keeping track of who owns wealth, and facilitating transactions from one person to another.

Let's draw a parallel with another human invention: writing. Writing's purpose is to record ideas so they can be read later. Ideas can be recorded by carving on a stone tablet, inking marks with a quill onto paper, using a typewriter, or through a word processor on a computer.

The typewriter was an amazing invention when it first came along - it made writing faster, and typewritten words were much easier to read than handwriting. But today, the typewriter is obsolete. Computers never run out of ink, they have a backspace button, and they can cut, copy, and paste text. Almost no modern writers cling to typewriters, except for decoration. Writers use the best available technology to do their work.

Similarly, at various stages of history, money's purpose has been fulfilled using giant stones, salt, gold, and banknotes. Banknotes are not the only form that money has taken, nor are they necessarily money's ultimate, final form. Banknotes might end up like the typewriter - a step on the evolutionary path.

Money is a technology, and as with any technology, if something better or cheaper comes along, then - as with the transition from typewriter to computer - the new technology could supplant the old one.

Fiat Money

Government-issued money is also known as **fiat money**. Conduct a Google search for: "what does fiat mean?", and the following definition is displayed:

fiat

/ˈfiːat, ˈfʌɪat/ ◀))

noun
noun: **fiat**; plural noun: **fiats**

a formal authorization or proposition; a decree.
"the reforms left most prices fixed by government fiat"

· an arbitrary order.

As this definition suggests, fiat currency is considered money due to "an arbitrary order" - it is money because the government says it is. Anyone who draws a banknote out from their wallet may see the words "legal tender" written somewhere. This term means that the issuing government has committed to let the bearer pay taxes with it, use it to settle fines, and pay for licenses and permits which the government issues.

But just because the government has "decreed" that it will accept fiat money doesn't mean everyone else must use it. For instance, transactions in the United Kingdom are settled with British pounds - but there is nothing to stop a buyer from handing over gold, or a giant stone, or Bitcoin, so long as the shopkeeper is happy to accept it. Any method can be used to settle a payment between two parties, provided that both leave the transaction feeling satisfied.

If People Trust It, It Is Real

The form that money takes is less important than the shared social agreement that it represents. Ask yourself - why is gold valuable? Yes, gold has practical uses. Yes, gold is rare, and digging it out of the ground is difficult. But much more importantly, gold is valuable because there is a collective social agreement among people. Gold is valuable because other people think gold is valuable.

If enough people believe gold has value, then it does. The same is true of fiat money and Bitcoin. If you trust the government and banks, you trust fiat money. But according to the 2017 Gallup News poll of Americans, just 12% of respondents said they trust Congress and only 32% said they trust banks.[8]

[9] There is room for an alternative.

Could Bitcoin Act As Money?

For something to act as money, it should be able to satisfy the below eight criteria.

1. Unit of account
2. Durable
3. Divisible
4. Portable
5. Fungible
6. Scarce
7. Medium of exchange
8. Store of value

Let's run through that list and see how Bitcoin fares.

1. **Unit of account?** Yes. Bitcoin is quantified numerically and is easily counted.
2. **Durable?** Yes. Bitcoin is software code and therefore lasts forever. Bitcoin is free from wear and tear.
3. **Divisible?** Yes. 1 Bitcoin can be divided into 100 million (or 0.00000001 Bitcoin). Even though 1 Bitcoin is now worth thousands of dollars, the smallest denomination of Bitcoin is smaller than the value of a penny. It is highly divisible.
4. **Portable?** Yes. Digital currencies like Bitcoin are even easier to move than cash and gold. Bitcoin can be shifted around the world in mere minutes and at very low cost.
5. **Fungible?** Yes. One person's Bitcoin is no more or less valuable than another person's.
6. **Scarce?** Yes. There will only ever be a finite number of Bitcoins issued, and earning newly issued Bitcoin requires expending computer resources and electricity through a process called "mining", which will be explained in a later chapter.
7. **Medium of exchange?** Yes. As long as people are happy to accept it, then Bitcoin can function as a medium of exchange. Thousands of people around the world are already trading real goods and services for Bitcoin every single day.
8. **Store of value?** Bitcoin's price is certainly quite volatile versus fiat currencies, leading to a reluctance to use Bitcoin as a store of value. But

Bitcoin is no different than gold in this respect. Gold's price also fluctuates when denominated in fiat currency, but the gold ingot doesn't change.

It is always difficult to trust new technology at first. Those who are old enough to remember life before the Internet may recall warily making their very first payment through online banking. Back then, there were all sorts of questions. *Is it safe? Will it work? Will the money disappear in a puff of smoke?* Before making that first payment, it was all very uncertain.

Once the "send" button was clicked, the user might have fallen into a panic, half-expecting that their worst fears would be realized and their payment would fall into some unrecoverable corner of cyberspace. However, once they became satisfied that they could trust it, online banking quickly became normal. Similarly, people's trust with Bitcoin will grow with experience.

* * *

Bitcoin runs through a **distributed ledger** called the **blockchain**.[10] By the time this chapter is finished, you will confidently understand what these words mean.

Distributed Ledger

Money is, in essence, a ledger. Each person's bank balance shows how much wealth they own. The previous chapter's story of the villagers on the island showed that it is essential for social groups to have a way of keeping track of money. Banks have traditionally filled this role by keeping a central ledger, but such a system results in the kinds of problems that come with trusted third parties.

By contrast, the distributed ledger that Bitcoin runs isn't stored in one single place, but on lots of different computers, all over the world, all at once. Bitcoin thus replaces the need for a bank by instead giving every member of the network a copy of the ledger. There are no central points of control. The system instead relies on the consensus of the network as a whole.

The validity of a transaction is by majority vote of the miners on the network. Mining will be explained more fully in a later chapter, but for now, think of miners as the replacement for the banks.

The Blockchain

Bitcoin's core innovation, which distinguished it from all earlier attempts to replace trusted third parties, is the blockchain. About every 10 minutes, Bitcoin miners create a new **block** of transactions data - consisting of people sending and receiving Bitcoin to each other over the preceding 10 minute period. A transaction is "confirmed" once miners add it to a block, and the block makes it onto the blockchain.

The verification of the transactions that make up the blocks is done through the collective work of the miners. These blocks are arranged in a chronologically ordered chain - hence "blockchain".

As new blocks are added to the blockchain, the amount of Bitcoin associated with each address is updated (a process further described in the next chapter). Once this happens, the computers in the network accept the new blockchain as a true and fair picture of the state of the ledger. This decentralized architecture removes the need for a trusted third party. Miners, not banks, update the ledger.

One of the most important things about the blockchain is that it is **immutable**. Once added, a transaction cannot be changed. Think of it as being like pages of an old written accounting ledger book. Once written in ink, it is indelibly there, forever.

* * *

The next chapter explores how the blockchain handles the individual addresses, and helps you conceptually understand crypto wallets and keys.

Understand Crypto Wallets & Keys

Cryptography is essential to several features of crypto, including privacy, security, and the ability to verify that all transactions are valid. The problem cryptography tries to solve is: *how is it possible to send a message between two parties, securely, without it getting intercepted or censored?*

For example, let's say James wanted to send the message "Hello" to Mary. One way of doing it is to use a secret code. As a simple example, imagine a code which dictated:

H = 7 e = k l = F l = F o = 1

That being the case, when James encrypted the word "Hello", it would result in the text "7kFF1". Then, Mary could decode it according to the same schedule in reverse and understand James' message.

However, the decoding schedule presents a problem. Say that James sent the same decoding schedule to Tom to securely communicate with him. But then Mary could listen in and understand private encrypted messages between James and Tom.

Asymmetric key cryptography solves this problem by having two coding devices for each person: a "public key" to encrypt a message, and a "private key" to decrypt any message which was encrypted with the corresponding public key.

James can <u>send</u> an encrypted message to Tom by using Tom's public key. But only Tom can <u>read</u> the message, which he does by using his private key. Mary doesn't have Tom's private key, so she cannot understand what was broadcast.

These public keys and private keys are generated through taking a large random number and running it through a key generation program. Then, the private key is used to derive the public key. The two resulting keys are mathematically linked to each other, but not in a way that makes it possible to backsolve what the private key is from knowing the public key.

A More Practical Explanation

It may be easier to think of cryptographic **keys** as similar to bank cards which allow people to call upon their stored money, and the crypto **wallet** as performing the same function as that of a physical leather wallet - a convenient place to keep all the bank cards together. Just as a person might have several bank cards inside their physical leather wallet, one crypto wallet can hold multiple cryptographic keys.

Cryptographic keys are long strings of seemingly-random letters and numbers. Only incredible memory experts could reliably memorize a series such as:

"19Vv7GD9rq3dF7UTKMyGq7EV5ADrRWQk2e".[11]

That's where crypto wallets come in, organizing the cryptographic keys in a way which is more legible to humans.

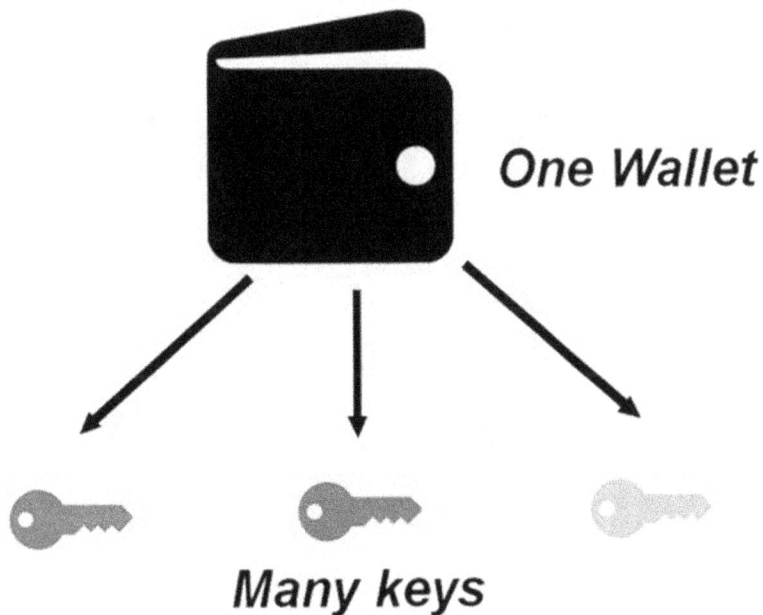

One Wallet

Many keys

Public Keys vs. Private Keys

Cryptographic keys come in pairs: the public key and the private key. The public key is needed to <u>receive</u> crypto from another address, and the private key is required to <u>send</u> crypto to another address.

- The **public key** is like a bank account number. Anyone can give it out freely, or even post it on the Internet for all to see. There is no risk - a person who only has possession of the bank account number (and not the password) can make deposits but cannot make withdrawals. The same is true for public keys.

- The **private key** is more akin to an Internet banking password. If a thief were to discover an Internet banking password, they might be able to steal the money inside the bank account. That is why no one should give out their Internet banking password to <u>anyone</u>. Actually, the private key must be protected even more carefully than an Internet banking password, because it is the <u>only</u> thing a thief needs. The private key is enough, by itself, to unlock all the crypto in that address. Unlike in the traditional banking system, there are no additional safeguards or the ability to reverse the transaction.

It is possible to represent an address with a **QR code**, which is a sort of square barcode similar to the one pictured below. This one has been smudged to protect anyone from accidentally sending payments to it, but it bears a close enough resemblance for you to know a QR code when you see one.

QR codes are convenient because they allow others to use a scanner to make a transfer instead of needing to deal with that long, convoluted series of letters and numbers such as:
"19Vv7GD9rq3dF7UTKMyGq7EV5ADrRWQk2f". Manually typing in such a string of characters is tedious and prone to error.

QR codes can be posted in any public place - for instance, on a website or at a shop counter. Once displayed, anyone can freely send payments to the address it is associated with.

Like Bank Cards, But Different

Bank accounts are denominated in a single currency (US dollars, euros, British pounds, etc.). Similarly, crypto keys are specific to a certain crypto token. Dealing in Bitcoin, Ethereum, and Litecoin requires three separate keys. A Bitcoin address can be used to receive Bitcoin, hold Bitcoin, and make a payment of Bitcoin, but cannot be used to do any of that with Ethereum, Litecoin, or other crypto tokens.

There is one important difference from bank cards - no identifying information is attached to cryptographic keys. Crypto doesn't care about name, address, social security number, date of birth, country of residence, or anything else. Whereas banks have the power to approve or deny an application based on the information they demand, crypto keys don't discriminate. Anyone with an Internet connection can get a cryptographic key.

Hot Wallets vs. Cold Wallets

Various wallets have different degrees of Internet connectivity. Broadly speaking, more Internet access equals greater convenience, but less security (and vice versa).

- A **hot wallet** is a crypto wallet <u>with</u> Internet access. These are necessary for facilitating movements of crypto, such as making payments, and trading on crypto exchanges.
- A **cold wallet** is a crypto wallet <u>without</u> Internet access. This gives them greater protection against the threat of computer hacking, but their lack of connectivity also reduces their accessibility to the true owner.

A good rule of thumb is to treat the crypto value stored in hot wallets in the same way as cash in a physical leather wallet. Keep only day-to-day spending needs in hot wallets, while retaining the vast majority of wealth in cold wallets. It would not be smart to walk around carrying $10,000 in cash. Better to carry just a little cash and keep the rest stored somewhere more secure. Then, when more is needed for day-to-day use, make a transfer from the secure place (cold wallet) to the convenient place (hot wallet).

Any crypto held on online crypto exchanges is in hot wallets. While the top exchanges all claim to have implemented best-practice security, one can never be too careful. SatoshiLabs (the creator of the popular Trezor wallet) has this to say about security at the crypto exchanges: "It is true that the quality of crypto services has improved significantly in the last years.

Nevertheless, third parties like crypto exchanges are always at risk of having severe security issues. Users have to trust that these online services indeed do what they claim. Users have to believe that an insider or a hacker cannot successfully attack these centralized services. More seriously, users can also be locked out of their exchange account by fringe regulation or direct government attack. The longer a user stores their funds in an exchange account, the bigger the risk. For this reason, it is recommended not to expose funds at exchanges for longer than necessary."

Anything stored on an exchange is at potential risk of being compromised. This is not a hypothetical fear - hackers allegedly reached in and stole hundreds of thousands of Bitcoins from the Mt. Gox online crypto exchange.[12] Mt. Gox subsequently filed for bankruptcy, leaving the rightful holders of those Bitcoins out of pocket. Unfortunately, there is little chance of recovery.

Different Types of Crypto Wallets

There isn't a single best crypto wallet for every need. Let's look at the different options, and the pros and cons of each. The below alternatives are roughly ordered from hot to cold.

1. Online Exchange Wallet (Very Hot)

Many online crypto exchanges allow users to store their crypto with wallets they provide. Doing so means that instead of dealing with (complicated-sounding) cryptographic private keys, users are able to log in to the online crypto exchange with a username and password - a refreshingly familiar user experience for crypto newcomers.

Storing crypto on an exchange means users may never see their private key. Instead, the exchange holds it on their behalf. This fact has critical security implications - remember, whoever holds the private key effectively has full control over all the crypto it is associated with. Think of the private key as being like cash - whoever holds it, owns it.

When users store crypto on an exchange wallet, they are delegating the responsibility of their private key to the exchange. There are advantages to this: the exchanges offer recovery in the event of a user losing or forgetting their password, which is not possible if users hold their own private key (unless they use a hardware wallet - see option #6 on this list).

However, turning over control of their private key to an online crypto exchange carries different risks; the exchange could potentially freeze the wallet, or the exchange itself could suffer a security breach, like Mt. Gox did. Anytime a user doesn't hold their own private key, these sorts of third-party risks exist. For these reasons, it is not advisable to hold substantial value on an online crypto exchange wallet.

2. Desktop Wallet (Hot)

Desktop wallets are software that runs on a personal computer. They allow users to view their crypto holdings and control their own private key without relying on a third-party exchange.

The developers of the various crypto tokens have created their own desktop wallets, which you can download for free. Examples include:
- **Bitcoin**: Bitcoin Core Wallet
- **Ethereum**: Ethereum Wallet
- **Litecoin**: Litecoin-QT

Additionally, other companies have developed multi-crypto desktop wallets, offering the convenience of showing users their entire crypto portfolio rather than needing separate desktop wallets for each of the various tokens they own.

There are dozens of desktop wallets with varying degrees of security and sophistication. But, a word of warning: before using a desktop wallet to store valuable crypto, it is essential to make sure the desktop wallet doesn't itself contain any malware.

You might not have the technical know-how to make this evaluation for yourself, so the best way to become confident about the security of a desktop wallet is to use only the ones that the crypto tokens have endorsed. Their developer teams independently verify the security of desktop wallets and check for vulnerabilities. Get access to a list of software wallets that the most popular crypto tokens recommend at **www.nathanrose.me/crypto**. It is better to use these.

3. Mobile Wallet (Hot)

Mobile wallets are similar to desktop wallets but are accessed through a mobile device instead of a personal computer.

The more limited memory space of a mobile device means that mobile wallets are smaller and simpler than desktop wallets. Mobile wallets are particularly convenient for making transactions at a store using a QR code. Make sure to apply the same security considerations as mentioned in the section on desktop wallets when considering which mobile wallet to use. Again, find links to the latest recommended mobile wallets at **www.nathanrose.me/crypto**

4. Digital File Wallet (Cold)

It is possible to create a file with the private key written inside and store it on a USB drive or a computer without a modem. For security, keep that device password-protected, and make the file password-protected too. Then, create backups of this file on a few other secure devices.

The crypto is lost if the private key is stored on only one device, and that device stops working, which is exactly what happened to a man from Australia who mined Bitcoin in 2009. Back then, each Bitcoin was worth just a few cents, and an ordinary personal computer could mine several Bitcoins per day, even without specialized mining hardware. After the novelty of mining thousands of near-worthless Bitcoins wore off, the man removed the mining program and put the private key for his thousands of Bitcoins onto a USB drive. By late 2013, the price of Bitcoin had skyrocketed to close to US$1,000 per unit, and the man thought his treasure trove of Bitcoins was worth millions. But tragically, his USB drive with the private key had died. "It was one of those cheap made-in-China ones… worst mistake of my life," he lamented.[13] Now his Bitcoins are lost forever, and there's <u>nothing</u> he can do about it.

It is easier to keep a single device secure, but there is a high risk of loss if that single device stops working. The risk of malfunction is significantly mitigated if there are several copies of the private key, kept in different places. Just remember that the crypto can be stolen if <u>any</u> of those copies fall into the wrong hands - so they <u>all</u> need to be securely held.

5. Paper Wallet (Very Cold)

Another option is to take a pen and write out the private key the old-fashioned way: on a piece of paper. Once that is done, it is essential to make sure that piece of paper is kept somewhere extremely secure, such as in a safe deposit box. At the risk of laboring the point - if a thief gets hold of the private key, they can transfer the crypto away to their own address.

Paper eliminates the possibility of electronic failure, but it is much less secure in the event of someone discovering the piece of paper. Electronic storage with password protection provides an extra layer of security in the event of someone stealing the device, whereas if someone gets hold of the paper, the private key is right there in black and white.

Again, it is essential to keep backups. As Javvy CEO Brandon Elliott warns, "It is crucial to keep that paper under lock and key in a <u>waterproof</u> and <u>fireproof</u> safe. Otherwise the 'dog ate it' excuse won't fly when trying to retrieve one's crypto." Keep copies of the paper wallet in different secure places to prevent the risk of all copies getting lost or destroyed.

You can create a paper wallet for Bitcoin at low cost using **www.bitcoinpaperwallet.com**. The website is user-friendly and features some handy videos and extra security advice (example: print the paper wallet in a private place, to ensure that no one sees the private key while it is being generated). There is even the option to purchase tamper-proof seals for a nominal fee - payable with either Bitcoin or PayPal.

6. Hardware Wallet (Very Cold)

Innovative companies have been able to mitigate the risks of other cold wallet storage options while also retaining the security advantages. These **hardware wallets** resemble a USB device and plug into a desktop computer's USB port. They have a price tag of around US$50-$100 and represent the overall best solution for long-term crypto storage. Anyone who comes to own significant quantities of crypto should invest in a high-quality hardware wallet.

Hardware wallets are still secure, even if the computer they are plugged into is connected to the Internet. KeepKey is one of the world's leading hardware wallets, and they explain how hardware wallets are walled off from any threat of external hacking: "Hardware wallets use encryption to communicate between the software on the computer and the firmware on the device. This allows private keys to never leave the hardware device. The software application sends the message to the device. Users confirm this information on the device, not the computer, and sign it with their private keys. Once the message has been signed, the software sends the message to the blockchain. Private keys do not move at any point in this process, which is why no information is confirmed on the computer."

If a hardware wallet is lost or destroyed, it is possible to safely recover the stored crypto using the recovery card that comes in the box with the hardware wallet. Various hardware wallets have different ways of handling this, but it is a bit like password recovery. These hardware wallets allow users to keep control of their own private keys while <u>also</u> having a form of recovery backup. It's the best of both worlds.

The top hardware wallets can handle multiple crypto tokens, though no hardware wallet can handle all of them. Before purchasing a hardware wallet, check that it supports the crypto tokens you want to hold.

Download a list of the latest recommended hardware wallets at **www.nathanrose.me/crypto**

* * *

It is fine to use any of the above wallet options while there is little value at stake. An online exchange wallet (option #1 from the above list) is the easiest to get started with, but users should take security more seriously when they invest more. Get several wallets - some for convenience, others for long-term storage, and none which hold everything. As the old saying goes, "Don't put all your eggs in one basket".

Now that we have covered the basics of how crypto works, let us move on to how to acquire it. In the next chapter, we will deal with the first method: mining.

What Happens In Proof-Of-Work Mining

There are three ways to acquire crypto:
1. Earning it through supporting the network (mining)
2. Buying it from someone else in exchange for ordinary cash
3. Getting paid with it in exchange for goods and services

This chapter concerns the first method - **mining**. The word "mining" comes from an analogy of digging for gold: expending effort to try and get something valuable. Proof-of-work miners support the network and get rewarded for their efforts.

A Competitive Game Of Chance

Proof-of-work crypto mining is like playing a game of chance, with other competitors playing at the same time. Let's gain a better comprehension of how crypto mining works by first taking a trip to the circus.

Imagine a game where there are several upside-down cups, one of which conceals a ball. It costs a dollar to turn over a cup, so playing the game is costly. If the player correctly guesses which cup contains the ball, they win a prize. If there is no ball under the cup turned over, the player gets nothing. But if the prize is big enough - let's say a golden nugget - the player will be happy to play this game repeatedly because their uncommon big wins will outweigh their frequent small losses.

Now, let's imagine this cup-and-ball game on a massive scale, with a million cups concealing a thousand balls. This extended version also has an extra feature: there are lots of other players participating at the same time, and only the first player to find a ball wins the prize. The addition of extra players means that the game of chance has become <u>competitive</u>. You can probably already see that the optimal strategy for finding a ball before anyone else does (and thus winning the prize) is to become as fast as possible at turning over cups.

Everyone else playing the game knows this too. All the players are furiously turning over cups as quickly as they can, trying desperately to find the proverbial needle in a haystack. Some will turn over cups faster than others. The fast players have a better chance of winning the game than the slow ones, but the slowest cup-turner could still get lucky.

Eventually, after much frantic searching, someone will find a cup with a ball. Once they do, they yell out loudly and hold their precious quarry aloft for all to see: *I've found it! I've found a ball!* Although annoyed, all the other participants must acknowledge that yes, a ball has been found, and the finder is to be awarded the prize. Once the first ball is found, all the cups and balls are shuffled and the game starts again with whoever wants to keep playing.

There's one more thing to add to make the analogy with proof-of-work crypto mining complete: the circus ringmaster doesn't want to give out too many prizes, so he regulates the game. Every so often, the ringmaster times how fast the game is won. If the players are winning too quickly, he reduces the number of balls in play. For example, he could drop the total number of balls from 1,000 down to 500 while keeping the number of cups at 1 million, thereby increasing the difficulty. Or if it's already too difficult, and players are losing interest, the ringmaster can distribute more balls into the cups and make the game easier.

Back To Crypto Mining

Armed with this conceptual groundwork of the cup-and-ball game, we can now get into the nitty-gritty of what happens in crypto mining.

We have already described crypto as a shared, decentralized ledger. This ledger needs to be updated over time as people transact. In the traditional financial system, this is the banker's job. But there is no banker in crypto, so the software protocol gets the miners to play a competitive game of chance to win the privilege to effectively "be the banker".

Miners must earn this privilege anew every block (remember, "blocks" are those regular collections of all the transactions throughout the network - in Bitcoin's case, a block is created about every 10 minutes). Just as only the first one to find a ball under a cup gets the ringmaster's prize, only the first crypto miner to win the competitive game of chance gets to update the ledger and receive the reward.

The **block reward** is what the miners stand to receive if they win the competitive game of chance - equivalent to the golden nugget in the cup-and-ball game. The block reward varies between the different crypto tokens. As of 2018, the Bitcoin protocol gives out a block reward of 12.5 Bitcoin every block.

To repeat, only the first winner of the competitive game of chance gets this reward. The winning miner takes all, and the losing miners take nothing. But because the game is played every time a new block is created (about every 10 minutes, in Bitcoin's case), losers have a chance to try and win next time.

The reason the protocol forces this guessing game upon the miners is to give crypto **scarcity**. Crypto needs to be costly to earn, like gold, which is difficult to dig out of the ground. If gold were everywhere, and anyone could pick up as much of it as they liked, gold wouldn't hold much value, as it wouldn't be scarce. Scarcity is one of the defining characteristics for anything to have monetary value.

What Are The Miners Really Doing?

Now it's time to get technical. To get to the bottom of what is really going on in the mining game requires an understanding of hashing and hexadecimal. This is admittedly one of the trickier parts of the book - but we will try and take it slowly.

Let's start with **hashing.** This is a cryptographic process that turns any length of data into a hexadecimal number of a fixed length. **Hexadecimal** is base 16. Humans are most familiar with base 10, with the digits 0 through to 9. Hexadecimal adds 6 more digits, represented by letters:

- A = 10
- B = 11
- C = 12
- D = 13
- E = 14
- F = 15

A Bitcoin hash of letters and numbers is an extremely large number. For example, the hexadecimal number *7DE81* is exactly equivalent to *515,713* in base 10.

Bitcoin uses a hashing algorithm called **SHA-256** to turn text inputs into hexadecimal hash outputs. Here are some examples of inputs and hashed outputs:

Input: "The quick brown fox jumped over the lazy dog"

Hash Hexadecimal Output:
7D38B5CD25A2BAF85AD3BB5B9311383E671A8A142EB302B324D4A5F

Input: "I pay you 1 Bitcoin"

Hash Hexadecimal Output:
894084441302098FDF9CF1B775706297F28C4AEBF2EC9BBA77A764E46

Input: "I pay you 2 Bitcoin"

Hash Hexadecimal Output:
A7546DB1064CAD5DACF70C93E88B75349920F76995E844B5210C09DA

There are a few things to note about hash hexadecimal outputs:

- The input can be any length, but the length of the output remains the same. It is possible to translate a word or an entire book - regardless, the SHA-256 output will still be 64 characters long.
- Changing even a single digit in the input (e.g. changing the number from "1" to "2" in the last two examples) creates a <u>completely</u> different output. The hash hexadecimal outputs of the last two examples are not at all similar, even though the inputs were only one character different.
- Hashing is a one-way process. It is easy to take a given input and find its hash output, but it is computationally infeasible to go the other direction and take the hash and try and decode the message. When it comes to hashing, "you can't un-bake a cake".
- It is also computationally infeasible to create a hash with given characteristics. Before putting the input through the hashing algorithm, there is no way to tell anything about what will come out the other end as output.

Now, back to the crypto miners playing the competitive game of chance. In each block, the network protocol sets a **maximum threshold number**. It then asks the miners to take the transaction data of everyone transacting within the network and use this as input to create a hash hexadecimal output (which, remember, is also a number). Then, the miners need to check whether the hash hexadecimal output number they have found is below the network's maximum threshold number. If the miner's output number is below the threshold number, they have effectively "found a ball" and can claim their prize (the block reward). If not, they have "found a cup with no ball in it" and have to keep trying.

Let's put it another way using an explanation with more familiar base-10 decimal numbers (which are completely equivalent to hexadecimal). The Bitcoin network is saying to the miners, "Turn all the transactions over the last 10 minutes into a hash output, which must be less than a certain maximum threshold number".

If 50 million is the maximum threshold number, then a Bitcoin miner needs to find a hash output with all the transactions of less than 50 million. If they do - congratulations - they win the privilege of creating the next block in the blockchain, and collect the 12.5 Bitcoin block reward. If their hash output is above 50 million - sorry - try again.[14]

This is what the miners are doing. Miners gather the transaction data across the whole network over the last 10 minutes and turn it into a hexadecimal hash output number. The whole network's collective messages - all those "I pay you 1 Bitcoin" and "I pay you 2 Bitcoin" transactions taking place all over the world - are aggregated together, hashed, and checked against the threshold number.

The miners keep adjusting the input using something called a **nonce**, which is a single number unrelated to any transaction. The addition of this nonce will, however, change the entire hash output (as we saw before - changing a single digit of the input completely changes the hashed output).

There is no way for the miners to find a hash output number which is below the network's threshold number except through pure trial and error, just like the cup-and-ball game. The faster the computer processor can generate hashes, the more guesses they can make - but it's still a guessing game. It is computationally infeasible for a computer to bypass the need to play the guessing game.

So the miners keep hashing, millions of times, searching for a hashed output below the maximum threshold number that the protocol is asking for - akin to looking for balls under the cups. If a miner's guesswork finds a solution, that miner broadcasts their solution to the whole network - effectively like holding a ball aloft and shouting, *I won!* The winning miner then collects their block reward, the ledger is updated, and the game begins anew.

Then, every so often, the crypto network protocol adjusts the threshold number up or down to make the guessing game easier or harder for the miners. This ensures that the game isn't won too quickly or too slowly - just as the circus ringmaster adds or removes balls from the game to regulate the difficulty. Bitcoin tries to set the threshold number so that a block is created about once every 10 minutes.

As more miners join the network, finding a winning hash output becomes harder. Crypto mining is a **zero-sum game:** no matter how many miners try to mine for Bitcoin, there is only a certain, fixed block reward provided for each block. When a new miner joins, it stiffens the competition for everyone else.

* * *

The next chapter shows you how to join the game and start mining for yourself. But be forewarned - the competition is extremely fierce.

How To Start Crypto Mining

The previous chapter explained how the network provides an incentive for proof-of-work miners to dedicate their computer resources to help maintain the decentralized ledger.

Anyone who wants to try crypto mining for themselves needs to know that the barriers to entry are significant, especially for the largest crypto tokens like Bitcoin, Ethereum, and Litecoin. In the early days, anyone could fire up their computer and earn Bitcoin using nothing more powerful than their ordinary desktop computer. Anyone is still perfectly free to start mining Bitcoin like this, but the competition has now increased so much that it is practically impossible to earn anything worthwhile without an up-front investment of hundreds or even thousands of dollars.

Getting into crypto mining in a meaningful way now requires **GPUs** (graphics processing units - basically a graphics card), or **ASICs** (application-specific integrated circuits - specialized hardware designed to do nothing but the specific mining task, repeatedly).

Why Start Crypto Mining?

There are a few possible motivations to begin crypto mining. Participating can be a rather interesting hobby for those who enjoy tinkering with computers, as mining gives hands-on experience with the operation of the network. You may also choose to start mining for altruistic reasons - one of the most tangible ways to support crypto is through mining. Each computer that dedicates resources to the crypto community makes it stronger.

But the serious crypto miners are not participating as a pastime or out of the kindness of their hearts. To paraphrase the famous 18th-century economist Adam Smith: *it is not due to the benevolence of the crypto miner that they maintain the shared decentralized ledger, but from their regard to their own interest.*

Professional crypto miners are in this business for one reason alone: to make money. The Bitcoin network and others have grown so quickly due to the profit motive. Rather than relying on people devoting computer power out of charity, it has expanded thanks to the invisible hand of capitalism.

A profitable crypto mining operation is roughly analogous to a money printing press. Setting up computers to automatically mint money for their owners is, of course, a very appealing prospect and one which has attracted a lot of interest.

Before diving headfirst into crypto mining, you ought to spend a little while researching online. Type "crypto mining farm" into the search box and watch a few videos to see the competition. Look at the massive warehouses teeming with row upon row of whirring computers, all mining for crypto as fast as they can. They have technicians on-site 24 hours a day, 7 days a week. They have set up sophisticated cooling systems with air filters - all in an effort to squeeze a fraction more efficiency out of their operation. They also go to considerable trouble to locate themselves in places where the electricity is inexpensive. Access to cheap power explains why Iceland is home to some of the world's largest Bitcoin mining operations. Seeing how seriously the pros take it should get you in the right mindset. Although it's not impossible to make money, it definitely isn't easy either.

No matter how many miners join the network, there is only a fixed amount of new crypto available every block. Getting a share requires competing with these savvy, motivated operators who desperately want that crypto for themselves.

Know The Numbers

The specifics on how to mine each of the hundreds of different crypto tokens would be a book in its own right, and one which would quickly go out of date. But regardless of which token is being mined, the overarching principle to remember is to know the numbers.

A proof-of-work crypto miner's expected daily profitability can be expressed as follows:

$$\textbf{Daily Profit} = \textbf{H} / \textbf{N} * \textbf{Q} * \textbf{P} - \textbf{E} - \textbf{L} - \textbf{M}$$

H = the miner's Hash rate (the speed at which the computer is working. One "hash" is every time a miner tries to create a block - or "make a guess", as described in the previous chapter. Hash rate is measured as hash-per-second.)

N = the entire Network's hash rate

Q = <u>Q</u>uantity of crypto distributed daily to the entire network

P = <u>P</u>rice per crypto

E = cost of <u>E</u>lectricity

L = cost of <u>L</u>abor (time setting up and maintaining)

M = cost of <u>M</u>ining hardware (graphics cards, etc.)

The leftmost part of the above equation (H / N * Q * P) represents the income a crypto miner can expect to earn. The parts to the right (- E - L - M) are the costs.

The most profitable crypto miners have some kind of edge in their numbers. For example, college students have been known to get around the large power bills that crypto miners typically incur thanks to their dormitory room rent being inclusive of electricity, meaning they can get free energy at the college's expense. Large crypto miners have scale on their side - they can purchase what they need in bulk, at a discount. Large miners also tend to enjoy better access to the latest, fastest, and most energy-efficient mining hardware.

The Two Big Unknowns

Most parts of the mining profitability equation can be figured out with fairly good accuracy. There are two exceptions:

1. "P" (price per crypto)

As anyone who has followed crypto for even a short while will know, the price of crypto (when measured in fiat currency) can be volatile. Imagine making a large investment in mining hardware only for the crypto price to halve. This has happened many times throughout the brief history of crypto. Miners who were dealing with a thin profit margin at the old (higher) price will find their operation untenable at the new (lower) price. On the other hand, prices can also quickly jump, resulting in a surprise windfall. Whether the market price will go up, down, or sideways is impossible to know in advance, making price volatility an unavoidable fact of life for crypto miners.

2. "N" (entire network's hash rate)

There is a fixed number of tokens provided in each block, and the amount a miner can expect to earn is determined by their share of the total hash rate. To use round numbers, a miner who owns 2% of the hash rate can expect to receive 2% of the new tokens minted (on average, over the long run). But if the rest of the network collectively doubles its hash rate, while that of the individual miner stays the same, the latter's share of new tokens earned will drop to just 1%. Receiving only half the tokens while spending the same on costs will markedly shift the profitability equation. It is highly uncertain how much new mining power will appear in the coming months and years.

* * *

Fortunately, there is a force which somewhat mitigates these two unknowns - namely, an unfavorable change in one should result in a favorable change in the other. If the price per crypto falls, then some less-profitable miners should drop out, thus lowering the overall network hash rate. As these two effects work in opposition to each other, the miners that remain ought to be able to make up for the lower price per crypto by earning a greater number of them - at least in theory.

Crypto Mining Options

1. Solo Mining

Solo mining involves an individual setting up their mining operation and trying to win a block reward on their own. If mining Bitcoin, and the miner happens to beat everyone else and seal off a block successfully, they will be awarded a full 12.5 Bitcoin (as of 2018).

Getting started with solo mining requires downloading the core software of the crypto and selecting the "generate" option. Find a list of where to download the core mining software for various popular crypto tokens at **www.nathanrose.me/crypto**

Realistically, millions of dollars of investment are needed to set up a crypto mining farm to make solo mining tenable - at least for the largest crypto tokens. Unless a miner has an absolutely huge amount of hash power at their disposal, winning a block through solo mining is incredibly unlikely.

2. Mining Pools

Mining pools are groups of cooperating miners who combine their collective mining efforts and share in whatever is earned. Within a mining pool, it doesn't matter which computer is responsible for finding the winning block, as the payout is distributed based on the share of hash rate each miner contributes to the collective.

For example, if a miner were part of a mining pool and contributed 10% of the hash rate, then that miner would receive 10% of the crypto reward every time <u>any</u> computer in their mining pool wins a block reward.

Collectivizing effort through a mining pool smooths out the profits. Instead of the highly variable profitability profile inherent in solo mining, participants in a large mining pool can look forward to making some profit each week.

Access a list of popular mining pools at **www.nathanrose.me/crypto**

3. <u>Cloud Mining</u>

Cloud mining has similarities to joining a mining pool. Participants become part of a collective which shares in the mined tokens. The important difference is that someone signing up to cloud mining doesn't need to host any mining hardware themselves. The cloud mining organizers host the noisy, power-sucking computers and send their members a share of the tokens generated, collecting a fee along the way. Cloud mining can be a great option to quickly get started, without needing to make a large up-front hardware investment or gain the technical know-how to set it all up.

Unfortunately, cloud mining methods are often deliberately opaque. CryptoCompare provides reviews of cloud mining providers, and they have the following advice when choosing between them: "The most important thing to take into account is how old and reputable the company is. Companies like Genesis Mining and Hashflare have a long-standing reputation in the industry, while others do not. Cloud mining specifically is a risky venture if you don't know the company well, given that it's hard to prove if the company is legit or if they're running a Ponzi scheme."

It is wise to research the different cloud mining providers by looking for honest reviews from others.

Hardware Considerations

Anyone who participates in solo mining or a mining pool (option #1 or #2 in the above list) must acquire their own mining hardware. There are five critical data points to understand before placing an order.

1. Hash Rate

This is the speed that the mining hardware works at. The faster it works, the more earning potential there is. Hash rate is measured in hash per second (or mega hash per second, giga hash per second, etc.). The higher this number, the faster the hardware is working.

2. Energy Efficiency

The biggest ongoing cost of proof-of-work crypto mining is the electricity consumed. Even an incredibly fast piece of mining hardware will suffer from suboptimal profitability if it isn't energy-efficient. It is even possible for miners to spend more on electricity than they earn in crypto. Energy efficiency is measured in watts per giga hash. The lower this number, the more energy-efficient the hardware is.

3. Price

The up-front cost of the mining hardware also matters. The fastest, most energy-efficient mining setup could still be a poor investment if it is beyond your budget. Don't forget to consider shipping and any import taxes and setup costs before hitting the "buy" button.

4. Delivery Speed

How quickly will the mining hardware be delivered to your door? Beware pre-ordering mining hardware. As many dismayed buyers have found out, manufacturing delays crop up all too frequently if the hardware is not already in stock and ready to ship. As the network hash rate of the largest crypto tokens can grow quickly, a delivery delay of even a few weeks or months can be fatal to the profitability of a hardware purchase.

5. Reliability

Look for honest reviews from other users who have previously purchased the same item. If the hardware is exclusively available on the seller's own website, make sure to scour for neutral review websites and read what others have had to say about the product. If there are lots of complaints of the hardware failing, look elsewhere.

In addition to these, there are a few "softer" considerations. How user-friendly is the mining hardware to set up? How noisy is it while running? How much heat does it put out? Some crypto mining hardware runs as loud as a vacuum cleaner and can seriously increase the room temperature. This doesn't matter if the mining setup is kept somewhere that doesn't make a difference to the owner's personal comfort, but anyone who plans to do their crypto mining in a small apartment should think carefully about whether they can put up with a hot, buzzing machine in close proximity.

Finally, miners should factor in additional equipment to make the hardware run properly, possibly including:

- Cooling fans
- Special power cables
- Mounting racks

Exactly which extra equipment is necessary varies by the hardware purchased. Some units are self-cooled. Some don't require an external energy source because they are USB-powered. Anyone who wants to make money from crypto mining needs to have a strong appetite to understand all of this detail and the will to keep learning. Crypto mining is not a "set it and forget it" endeavor. The pros with the large-scale mining farms will do everything in their power to compete as hard as they can. Anyone who wants to keep up must also stay on top of their numbers and constantly optimize their setup.

Finally, before buying, decide between generalized and specialized hardware. ASIC cards are faster but are specific to one type of cryptographic algorithm - for instance, one ASIC card may be able to mine using SHA-256 (which Bitcoin uses) but may be incapable of switching to mine Ethereum or Litecoin because those tokens use different hashing algorithms. GPUs are able to switch but are slower (because they are not specialized). Those who are just getting started with crypto mining could find that a GPU is a better option because it allows them to experiment with mining several different crypto tokens and settle on which they like best.

* * *

Crypto mining is not the quickest or cheapest way to get crypto for the first time. Most people will find buying crypto from somebody else through an exchange to be a far easier way to get started. The next chapters deal with how to do that.

Online Crypto Exchanges

Here again are the three ways to acquire crypto:
1. Earning it through supporting the network (mining)
2. Buying it from someone else in exchange for ordinary cash
3. Getting paid with it in exchange for goods and services

This chapter deals with the second option. For crypto to fulfill its promise, the mainstream needs to adopt it. Not everyone is interested in setting up the complicated mining equipment described in the previous chapter. Fortunately, users can instead choose to buy crypto from someone else who already has some.

Buyers and sellers go to online crypto exchanges to meet and trade. There, they can trade between different crypto tokens (e.g. change Bitcoin for Ethereum) or between fiat money and crypto (e.g. trade US dollars for Bitcoin).

How Online Crypto Exchanges Work

Readers who are already familiar with stock trading platforms will be able to easily understand **online crypto exchanges**. They operate virtually identically, and even their interfaces look similar. But if online trading represents new territory, it may be helpful to think of an online crypto exchange as analogous to an open-air marketplace - the kind where stallkeepers set up shop and sell goods to passersby.

The sellers loudly cry out their prices for buyers to hear: *Fresh fish! $8 a kilogram!* Meanwhile, the adjacent stallkeeper is bellowing, *Get your fresh fish! One kilogram, $7.90!* Assuming uniform fish quality, well-informed buyers will prefer the lower-cost seller. Competition between the sellers ensures that buyers are at less risk of being overcharged. This is one of the reasons that marketplaces like these are so popular among buyers. Sellers enjoy the convenience of marketplaces too. They give sellers a single place to go, without needing to expend effort finding buyers for their wares. Both sellers and buyers do plenty of business, and everyone receives a fair price.

One important difference between these open-air bazaars and online crypto exchanges is that the crypto exchanges also have <u>buyers</u> openly offering prices. This is the equivalent of a buyer in the crowd shouting, *I'll buy a kilogram of fresh fish for $7.50! Any takers? Who will sell me fish for $7.50 a kilogram?* That buyer might find himself outbid by another fellow offering $7.60. Competition between buyers drives the price up at the same time as competition between sellers drives the price down. Eventually, a market price emerges somewhere in the middle.

Why Do We Need Crypto Exchanges?

Because of the significant up-front and ongoing costs involved, the biggest online crypto exchanges are for-profit enterprises. They charge fees to their users every time they trade. These fees go towards paying for the computer infrastructure, security systems, and the legal regulations governing their operation. None of this is free, and the online crypto exchanges want to make a profit too.

You may have already spotted an irony. Despite all the talk of crypto acting as a force for removing middlemen, the fee-charging, centralized exchanges still exist. The fees are low compared to the traditional financial system, but they nevertheless represent a departure from the fee-free, frictionless world that crypto purists would prefer.

Online crypto exchanges also reintroduce a data security risk due to the personal information the exchanges collect. Prominent cryptographer Nick Szabo put it this way: "Whereas the Bitcoin blockchain itself is probably the most secure financial network in existence (and indeed must remain far more secure than traditional payment networks in order to maintain its low governance costs and seamless cross-border capability), its peripheral services based on older, centralized web servers are very insecure."[15]

For their part, the exchanges argue that they are essential to making crypto more accessible to everyday people. Online crypto exchanges make buying and selling crypto more user-friendly, and give everyone a place to go to conduct trade - just like the open-air fish market. Regardless of their merits (or otherwise), you will probably want to use an online crypto exchange at some point. So let's move on to how to evaluate which to choose.

Online Crypto Exchange Choices

Life will be a lot easier if the right online crypto exchange is chosen up front. It is not a simple choice - the market is very fragmented. There are many providers, and their names often sound fairly similar to each other.

An overriding rule to keep in mind is: all else equal, it is usually better to use the larger exchanges. There are two main reasons why:

- Larger exchanges have greater **liquidity** (i.e. more buyers and sellers). Having liquidity is one of the most critical markers of a desirable exchange - more buyers and sellers means more competition and therefore a better market price.
- Larger exchanges are better resourced. This means they can offer stronger security, more responsive customer service, and a better website user experience.

The online crypto exchange landscape moves rapidly - exchanges frequently merge, open, close, and change their names. Rather than list the exchanges here in the book (which would quickly become outdated), I maintain and update a list of links to the large international online crypto exchanges. Access the list at **www.nathanrose.me/crypto**

Evaluating The Exchanges

Once you have downloaded the list of online crypto exchanges, you should use the following criteria to decide on your exchange of choice.

1. <u>Which Countries Are Supported?</u>

Certain exchanges are open or closed to different people, depending on their passport, residency, and country of banking. Some exchanges refuse Russian citizens. Some will lock out those living in certain states of the USA. Some will not take anyone who can't prove their address with a utility bill or bank statement.

If it isn't clear which countries a crypto exchange accepts, check their frequently asked questions or send them an email. It is common for newcomers to grow annoyed if their application gets rejected and abandon crypto because they decide it is too hard. Rather than suffer this frustration, you should get the information about whether or not you are eligible <u>before</u> filling in a time-consuming application form.

2. <u>Are Fiat Currency Transfers Possible?</u>

Some exchanges point-blank refuse to support fiat money deposits. By keeping themselves restricted to the crypto ecosystem, these exchanges save themselves significant regulatory headaches but are incapable of facilitating trades between crypto and fiat money. Those who are buying into crypto for the first time <u>need</u> to use fiat money to buy crypto, so make sure that the exchange supports this.

3. <u>Which Tokens Are Supported?</u>

No exchange offers all crypto tokens. Practically every exchange supports Bitcoin, but buying other tokens requires finding out whether the exchange supports them or not. Go to the website of an exchange and look at which crypto tokens they offer markets in, or visit the crypto token's website where they often list the exchanges that offer it as an option. Access a list of the most widely-traded crypto tokens at **www.nathanrose.me/crypto**

4. <u>Which Trading Pairs Are Supported?</u>

The fewer trades required to make the desired transaction, the easier and cheaper it tends to be. It is like air travel - flying direct from origin to destination is far preferable to having a layover at another airport.

For example, if an investor holds euros and wants to use them to buy Litecoin, ideally the investor will find an exchange which allows that trade directly with a euro / Litecoin market. The investor should avoid, if possible, needing to go through two or more steps to get between the current position and the desired position. It is more hassle to have to first trade euros for Bitcoin, and then trade Bitcoin for Litecoin. Also, by doing two trades, users get hit by fees twice.

If the user's fiat money is in a less widely supported currency (for instance, New Zealand dollars), they will probably need to make a transfer into a more widely supported currency, such US dollars, before being able to trade.

5. <u>What Are The Fees?</u>

Pay careful attention to the exchange fees, as they can become expensive if a user is not cautious. The more the exchange takes, the less money stays in the pocket of the investor. Divide the fees being charged by the starting amount to see how much the exchange is taking (as a percentage). Common fees include:

- Deposit fees: Some exchanges charge a per-deposit fee to discourage frequent, small deposits and encourage fewer, large deposits. To further encourage large deposits, the exchange may not charge a fee for deposits above a certain threshold.

- Trading fees: These are the main fees that crypto exchanges impose to make their money - every time a trade goes through, a percentage of the transaction value is paid to the exchange.
- Miner fees: Paid to the network to encourage the transaction to be appended more quickly to the next block. A higher fee gives the user a quicker confirmation of their transaction. This fee does not go to the exchange, but some exchanges have higher mining fees than others because they want to have their transactions settled onto the blockchain as quickly as possible. Other exchanges allow users to choose their own mining fees, giving them the option to pay less if they don't mind their transaction taking a bit longer to clear.

6. Is The Exchange Large & Liquid?

Returning to the fish market - if the best price for buying fish was $7.60, and the best price for selling fish was $7.90, then a $0.30 gap would exist. In financial markets, this gap is known as the **bid-ask spread.** Anyone who wants to buy or sell a fish immediately must cross this divide and accept the best price others are offering. As in:

- *Okay, I will buy your fish for $7.90,* or
- *Fine, I will sell my fish for $7.60.*

Greater liquidity reduces the bid-ask spread, resulting in a higher price for sellers and a lower price for buyers. Exchanges with excellent liquidity have a minimal difference between how much it costs to buy crypto on-market and how much is received by selling.

The **round-trip cost** combines the explicit fees, together with the cost a trader is exposed to through the bid-ask spread, to give a single measure of how costly it is to trade on an exchange. To calculate the round-trip cost, take the value of crypto purchasable at the current market price (net of fees), less the proceeds from selling the same amount (net of fees), divided by the total starting amount.

Here is a worked example:

- An investor starts with $1,000 to invest in Litecoin.
- The "ask" is $244.80 per Litecoin (the price sellers are demanding).

- The "bid" is $243.10 per Litecoin (the price buyers are willing to pay).
- The exchange takes a fee of 0.2% per trade.

Buying in:

$1,000 x 99.8% = $998 to spend, net of transaction fees

$998 / $244.80 = 4.0768 Litecoin purchased

Selling out:

4.0768 Litecoin x $243.10 = $991.07 (before fees)

$991.07 x 99.8% = $989.09 received (after fees)

Round-trip cost:

$1,000 - $989.09 = $10.91

$10.91 / $1,000 = 1.09% round-trip cost

7. What Is Their Security Reputation?

Do an online search for the name of the online crypto exchange along with the words "hack" or "security breach", and it will return results which may influence the decision over whether to use the exchange under consideration. Remember, larger, better-resourced exchanges are preferable because they usually have stronger security measures in place.

8. What Is The User Interface Like?

The user interface of the online crypto exchange is a matter of personal preference. Some enjoy the simplicity of an exchange which looks and feels like online banking. Others favor the superior functionality of something that resembles a foreign exchange trading platform. Adding more options and more crypto tokens naturally makes the interface more intimidating to beginners, but more advanced users will desire more powerful options.

9. Other Services

Some exchanges offer extras beyond the ability to buy and sell crypto. These include:

- Payment Applications: some exchanges have a built-in payments app allowing users to easily access their exchange balance and make payments using a mobile device.
- Margin Trading: margin trading enables users to amplify their risk exposure using borrowed money. In a simple example, an investor could

put up 50% of the collateral in a trade, and the exchange could put up the other 50%. In this scenario, a 10% rise in the price of Bitcoin would increase their investment by 20% (conversely, a 10% fall in price would reduce their investment by 20%). Margin trading with crypto is not for the fainthearted. You should get some experience and make sure you know what you are doing before margin trading.

- Cloud Mining: certain exchanges facilitate cloud mining (described in the previous chapter) right there on the exchange platform.

* * *

If you do not get accepted onto the first exchange you try, don't fret. This happens to a lot of people. As the next chapter covers, the sign-up process can take some patience.

Fortunately, users do not need to decide upon just a single crypto exchange. In fact, it is very advisable to have multiple exchange accounts. Exchanges offer free sign-up, so it makes sense to have options. Different exchanges do different things better, and it pays to have a backup exchange in case one of them has an outage.

Once you choose which platform(s) you prefer, you will need to apply to join. The sign-up and verification process is covered in the next chapter.

Exchange Sign-up Process

This chapter explains how to sign up to an online crypto exchange. Following these step-by-step instructions should save you from the annoyance of having your verification application rejected.

Incoming Red Tape

As many exasperated users will attest, the experience of signing up to an online crypto exchange can be fraught with difficulty. Crypto is borderless and open to anyone - but most online crypto exchanges are firmly mired in a world where borders matter, bureaucracy abounds, and gatekeepers get to decide who gets an account and who doesn't.

Coinmama helps users buy Bitcoin and Ethereum using a credit card. Their view on third-party exchanges is as follows: "In order to get from today's world of bank accounts and cash to a world in which everyone is in complete control over their own finances, the reality is that we need to comply with both regulations. However, going forward, more and more value will change hands through the blockchain, which means we'll see a steady transition towards greater anonymity. We don't think regulation will ever go away completely (and that's a good thing), but it will be a big step in the right direction."

Here is the distinction: crypto <u>itself</u> is borderless and open to all, but the online crypto <u>exchanges</u> are not. As long as transactions stay denominated in crypto, expect the system to work as advertised, with low-cost, fast execution and no restrictions concerning who can send and receive money. Only when users transfer fiat money in and out with their bank accounts are regulations reintroduced. It is worth noting that none of this is a problem if crypto is acquired through mining, or if crypto is directly received as payment for goods or services. It only becomes difficult if a bank account is involved somewhere.

Online crypto exchanges always face an uphill battle to get a bank account for themselves. Compliance officers at banks are naturally risk-averse - the default position when something outside the box crosses their desk is to say "no". To get a "yes", the online crypto exchange is forced to collect the same information from their customers that the banks themselves would gather in order to comply with their own Know Your Customer (KYC) and Anti-Money Laundering (AML) requirements.

Therefore, the issue isn't really with crypto but rather with the banking system. All the red tape is a good reminder - if one were needed - of what motivated the original crypto pioneers in the first place.

The Sign-up & Verification Steps

The sign-up and verification process involves paperwork and demands for proof of identity. Frequently, applications are rejected if they do not fit the strict standards imposed. But by following these steps, you will do everything in your power to ensure this does not happen to you.

1. <u>Enter Your Email Address & Create A Password</u>

Make sure that the password is unique and not easily guessed. It should not be a dictionary word, and it should use a combination of numbers, lowercase letters, uppercase letters, and symbols. Use a password management tool to generate a random password and securely store it for later use. I maintain an up-to-date list of password management tools on **www.nathanrose.me/crypto**

2. <u>Enable Basic Security</u>

Follow the prompts to get **Two-Factor Authentication** (2FA) enabled. This is the bare minimum security to have in place. 2FA involves downloading a smartphone app which generates a one-time code that changes every minute or so. The user's password stays the same, but to log in, the 2FA code is also required. The best app (for both Android and iPhone) is called "Google Authenticator", which is capable of storing all the 2FA codes from multiple exchanges all in one place.

3. <u>Upload Verification Documents</u>

Each crypto exchange has slightly different requirements, but documents to upload may include:

Identification document (e.g. passport, driver's license, government-issued ID card) - sometimes both the front and the back.
  • The date of birth and ID number are clearly visible.

- It must not have expired.
- Make sure that all the edges are visible.

Proof of address (e.g. bank statement, utility bill).
- It may need to be dated recently.
- Two forms of identification may be required.

A screenshot of the applicant.
- You may need to hold your identification document and / or a piece of paper showing the date and your signature.
- Keep a neutral expression (don't smile).
- Remove hats or anything obscuring the face.

Read the instructions provided by the exchange carefully, and do <u>exactly as required</u>. If asked to upload a .jpg image of no more than 2 megabytes, then make sure to send the exchange precisely this.

Also, take special care to ensure the information always matches up. If the identity document submitted says "Rebecca", then that is what should be typed in the "Name" field - even if the applicant normally goes by "Becky". If required to send two proofs of address, make sure they show exactly the same address as each other. Getting any of this wrong can be grounds for rejection. It sounds excruciating, and it is - but there is very little flexibility in these rules.

Run through the following checklist before submitting the identity verification:
- Images are clear (not blurry / out of focus).
- Photos are not too dark / have too much glare.
- No part of the image is cut off.
- Remember to attach an image of the back of the identification document (if requested).
- The document is valid (not expired).
- Fingers holding the identification are not obscuring any part of it.
- Not wearing sunglasses or a hat in the photo.

4. <u>Wait</u>

The exchange needs time to review the documents once submitted, and this needs to be done by a human. If they have a backlog of applications, there might be a wait of several days or even several weeks. Unfortunately, there is no way to speed up the process. This is why it is so important to submit the application to the online crypto exchange well in advance of when you want to start trading.

Many online crypto exchanges are fast-growing start-ups, struggling to keep pace with the load of applications coming their way. Compliance departments can become overwhelmed if too many people apply at once - which tends to happen especially when crypto has recently been experiencing rapid price increases.

It is a great idea to use the waiting time to sign up to other online crypto exchanges - that way, even if (despite your best efforts) you get rejected by one exchange, you still have the chance to get approved by others. You need to get approved by at least one exchange, so it is best to increase your odds by getting the clock ticking on more than one exchange at a time.

5. Receive Notification Of The Outcome

Once the exchange has checked the documents, a message will inform you whether you were approved or not. The bad news is, if rejected, you will have to start again. The compliance departments rarely explain <u>why</u> an application is turned down - often, all that is sent is "no".

If rejected, try another exchange, or resubmit to the exchange that sent the denial. Some exchanges have a stand-down period for failed applications - so it might be necessary to wait some days before being allowed to submit the documents to the same exchange again. This is why it is crucial to get the application as airtight as possible the first time around.

* * *

Armed with this advice, you should be able to find an online crypto exchange to approve you. But if, no matter what you try, none let you join, the chapter titled Alternative Ways To Acquire Crypto provides some backup options.

If your verification is approved with at least one exchange, you can get started with funding your account and use the exchange to buy your first crypto. That is the subject of the next chapter.

Buy Crypto On An Online Exchange

If you have successfully managed to sign up to an online crypto exchange, you are tantalizingly close to owning your first crypto! This chapter deals with the final steps. Whether or not to invest is completely up to you, but learning will proceed much faster if you invest real money - even if it is only a modest sum.

Account Funding

Fiat money must be deposited into the online crypto exchange account in order to use it to buy crypto. If you decide to invest, it is advisable to start with a small amount. Mistakes can happen when trying anything new. Only consider investing more after trying out an exchange with a smaller amount first.

Below are five possible ways to fund an exchange account with fiat money. Be aware that not all online crypto exchanges offer all funding options.

1. Local Bank Transfer

This is the fastest way to fund an account, if it is offered as an option. Depending on where you are located, you may be able to get a direct connection between your online crypto exchange account and your bank account. Getting a direct connection should be possible for most residents of the United States and the European Economic Area. Once it has been set up, you should simply make a transfer between your bank account and your online crypto exchange account.

2. International Bank Wire

If you live somewhere that doesn't offer a local banking link, then an international bank wire may be necessary. These wires attract quite hefty fees - exactly how much varies, but reckon on approximately US$30 per transaction. If the international bank wire requires a currency exchange (e.g. your bank balance is in Australian dollars, but the online crypto exchange deals only in US dollar deposits), then expect to be stung with a poor exchange rate as well.

International money transfers can seem intimidating at first. The crypto exchange will present a list of their details, and you must go to your online banking and enter this information along with the amount to send. It will likely include:

- Bank name
- Bank physical address
- Bank country
- Bank SWIFT code / BIC code
- Account name (fully spelled - no initials)
- Physical address (not a PO Box number)
- Account number
- Reference number (This must be included exactly as given. It matches the deposit to the user's account with the online crypto exchange.)

If in any doubt, ask for clarification before making the transfer. Once the international bank wire goes through, users must wait a few days before the funds are credited to their account on the online crypto exchange.

3. PayPal

PayPal offers great convenience, but make sure to keep track of the fees they charge. The foreign exchange rates from PayPal are often even worse than international bank wire exchange rates. Although the value lost through the exchange rate is higher with PayPal, PayPal at least tends to have a smaller fixed fee per transaction. Be aware of both the fixed fees _and_ the cost implicit in a poor exchange rate.

4. Credit Cards / Debit Cards

Using a credit card or debit card to buy crypto is another way to avoid the several-day wait that international bank wires suffer from. Again, be aware of the associated fees and look for the best deal.

This method requires entering the user's credit card information with the online crypto exchange, just as if making an online purchase. Log in to the exchange and click "Add a Credit / Debit Card" (if this is an option). Once approved, it will be possible to buy crypto using this linked card.

Some credit card issuers have started blocking crypto purchases. If this happens, try switching to a debit card instead.

5. <u>Alternative Money Transfer</u>

Fintech companies have set out to solve the problems of poor exchange rates, high fees, and slow transfers. They offer many of the same services as bank accounts but at a fraction of the cost. They are able to offer their services more cheaply because they do everything online and don't have the overheads of the traditional banks - they have no physical branches and far fewer staff.

Access to these accounts is constantly evolving. But if you can get an account with them or an equivalent service, the experience can be better than making an expensive international bank wire, PayPal transfer, or credit card payment.

Buying On The Exchange - First Time

Once the online crypto exchange account is funded, it is possible to trade that money for crypto. When trading, users have the option to be either a "price-maker" or a "price-taker".

Here is the difference:
- Price-makers <u>offer</u> prices to buy and sell at. These are known as **limit orders**.
- Price-takers <u>take</u> the best price offered by others. These are known as **market orders**.

Market orders are a better option for newcomers. A market order gives the best available price that others are offering, and the transaction will be completed immediately. The rest of *The Crypto Intro* will assume that you buy Bitcoin as your first crypto.

While logged in to the online crypto exchange, select "Bitcoin" and the "market order" option. Then, enter the amount of Bitcoin to buy, or the amount of fiat money to spend. Click "confirm", and the trade will execute instantly. At this point, you will be the proud owner of your first crypto!

Later, you may wish to experiment with limit orders. These are useful if there is a certain price you want to buy or sell at, as limit orders set things up such that the trade will execute automatically, but only if the market moves enough. For instance, if the market price of Bitcoin is currently US$10,000, a limit order could be created to sell at US$12,000 if the whole market shifts up to that higher level. The trade will not execute unless the price of Bitcoin rises to this level.

When placing limit orders, be very careful with the price inserted. If the prevailing price of Bitcoin is around US$10,000, and a limit sell order of US$1,000 is entered (i.e. carelessly leaving off a zero), then the user may be in big trouble. Their order could get filled immediately, their Bitcoin will be transferred out of their account, and the user will receive only 10% of the money they thought they were going to get. It might have been an honest mistake, but no one is going to undo it - least of all the overjoyed buyer. Some exchanges provide an alert if a trader submits a price which is drastically different from the market price, but ultimately the responsibility lies with whoever presses the "confirm" button. Therefore it is recommended to start with market orders before moving on to limit orders.

* * *

This concludes the series of chapters on choosing, signing up for, funding, and buying with online crypto exchanges. Next, we turn to other options for buying crypto apart from the online crypto exchanges. They are interesting even for readers who were able to get an online crypto exchange account. But they are even more essential for those who found getting approved either impossible or undesirable.

Alternative Ways To Acquire Crypto

There are two problems with most online crypto exchanges:

1. Not Everyone Can Get Approved

Many online crypto exchanges are highly regulated and demand that all new users undergo a background check. The exchanges then have the power to deny an account based on the information that applicants provide - exactly the sort of restriction that crypto was meant to do away with. Some people cannot prove identity, or are underage, or are from a country that the exchanges don't support. For them, the doors to enter an online crypto exchange remain bolted shut.

2. Exchanges Curtail Privacy

The data that online crypto exchanges collect can become a target. In February 2018, Coinbase was ordered to provide taxpayer ID, name, birth date, address, and historical transaction records for certain high-transacting customers.[16] Beyond the potential for government surveillance, hackers can also compromise the records of an online crypto exchange if their security is not tight. Using an online crypto exchange is a significant weak link for any user who wants anonymity.

If you struggled to sign up to an online crypto exchange, this chapter provides alternative options for you to acquire your first crypto.

LocalBitcoins

The website www.localbitcoins.com helps strangers to transact in Bitcoin with one another directly, avoiding online crypto exchanges. Here's how it works: users log in to LocalBitcoins and enter their location. Then, they can view the traders in their area offering to buy and sell Bitcoin. There are many payment options, including bank deposit, PayPal, and using cash in person. In-person cash transactions afford the maximum in universal access and anonymity.

LocalBitcoins displays the following information for traders registered on their site:

- Reputation score
- Maximum and minimum they will trade
- The price they offer to buy and sell at
- Where to meet

An in-person cash transaction using LocalBitcoins will look something like this: the Bitcoin buyer shows up with cash and destination wallet address while the Bitcoin seller arrives with a device with access to their Bitcoin wallet. The buyer will hand over the cash, and the seller will make a transfer of Bitcoin to the buyer's address. No banks or online crypto exchanges are involved, and the only record is on the blockchain - nothing identifying the buyer, seller, or why the transaction occurred.

Here are a few things to watch out for if you decide to trade in crypto through LocalBitcoins.

- Reputation: A trader's reputation score is a measure of how many people have used them before and the collective feedback that others have given in past dealings. If the crypto trader on LocalBitcoins already has hundreds of positive reviews, then it is fair to expect a similar positive experience, as no one wants to ruin their hard-earned reputation.
- Safety: Once the banks and online crypto exchanges have been left behind, the protections they afford are forfeited too. When dealing with substantial amounts of cash, it pays to be aware of personal security. Insist on meeting in a public place to minimize risks - even when dealing with traders with positive feedback scores.
- Price: One of the major disadvantages with in-person cash trades is that the prices offered are usually quite a bit worse than on the online crypto exchanges. There is less competition on LocalBitcoins than on centralized online marketplaces. Because meeting in person involves time and travel, the traders expect to be compensated for the inconvenience. Before trading, compare the price on LocalBitcoins with the price listed on the major online crypto exchanges to calculate the premium the trader is charging.

Meetup

Crypto get-togethers are regularly organized through www.meetup.com all over the world. After signing up on the website, users can enter their location and search for "Bitcoin", "crypto", and "cryptocurrency". So long as they are in a town of reasonable size, the calendar will likely have events coming up to meet other crypto enthusiasts.

Someone at the meeting will probably be willing to trade, especially to anyone buying for the first time. Most people in crypto want the community to grow, and will be all too happy to sell a little crypto to help a newcomer get started.

If Meetup isn't available nearby, try to find a friend who already owns crypto and is willing to sell some. Simply get the friend to send the crypto to the desired wallet address, and pay them in cash.

Gift Card Purchases

Another way around the online crypto exchange compliance procedures is to avoid fiat money entirely and deal in other instruments which still act like cash.

Several websites enable users to buy and sell Amazon gift cards using Bitcoin. Amazon is "the everything store", meaning Amazon gift cards can be used to purchase practically anything. There are less-developed marketplaces for other gift cards too, such as Apple iTunes cards.

The current list of gift-card purchase websites is at www.nathanrose.me/crypto

Credit Card Purchases

Services exist to enable the direct purchase of crypto using a credit card. These services charge about 5% on top of the value of crypto being bought. These websites often have a much simpler sign-up process than the online crypto exchanges. All that is required is an existing wallet address to send the purchased crypto to.

The websites enabling credit card purchases are always changing. An up-to-date list is available for download at www.nathanrose.me/crypto

* * *

Whether through an online crypto exchange as described in the previous chapters, or the alternative options outlined in this chapter, there is a way of acquiring crypto for everyone. If the first method tried doesn't work, try another. With persistence, you will get your first crypto.

The next chapter finally moves on to the fun stuff: using crypto to buy real goods and services and starting to accept crypto as payment.

Sending & Receiving Payments

Returning to the three ways of acquiring crypto:

1. Earning it through supporting the network (mining)
2. Buying it from someone else in exchange for ordinary cash
3. Getting paid with it in exchange for goods and services

It is time for number three on the list - sending and receiving payments. By now, you should have both a wallet and your first crypto. Let's now test the system out and make a transfer from one wallet to another.

Send A Payment To Yourself

By sending a payment to yourself, you can experience what it feels like to both send <u>and</u> receive a payment.

Create a new wallet address with the website **www.blockchain.com**. Click "Get A Free Wallet" and follow the self-explanatory sign-up steps. blockchain.com is <u>not</u> an online crypto exchange - it <u>just</u> provides a crypto wallet, and does not offer trading between fiat and crypto. This means that blockchain.com does not collect as much information from the user. You should be up and running in a few minutes.

Once the account has been approved, log in to the blockchain.com dashboard and select the crypto token that you already own in your other wallet (such as at the online crypto exchange, if you were able to get approved). If you already own Bitcoin, select that.

Next, click "Request" as pictured in the below diagram.

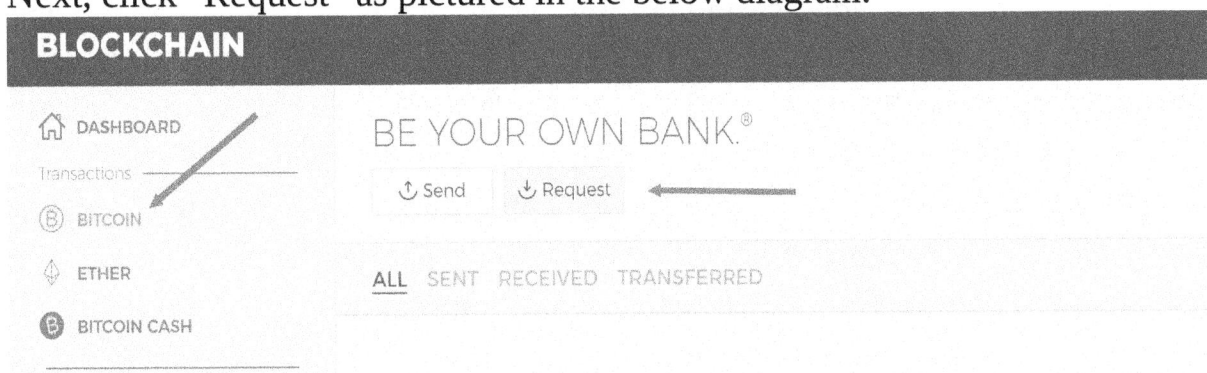

The next screen will resemble the below, with a unique string of jumbled numbers and letters. In the screenshot below, the address has been blurred, but it will look something like (but NOT exactly): "19Vv7GD9rq3dF7UTKMyGq7EV5ADrRWQk2e". Whatever it says on your screen is your address. To emphasize - DON'T use the string of numbers and letters written here inside the book!

You need to take that address and copy it. Then, when you have logged back in to your other wallet (such as at the online crypto exchange), select "Send" and enter the blockchain.com address as the destination. Try sending a little Bitcoin from your first wallet to your new wallet at blockchain.com.

It will take a few minutes to go through - Bitcoin payments are not instant, but it will almost certainly take less than an hour. The online crypto exchange may send a notification email to let you know once the transaction is complete.

Once the Bitcoin has turned up in your wallet with blockchain.com, try repeating the same steps in the other direction - i.e. sending some Bitcoin from your blockchain.com wallet back to your first wallet, to make sure that everything is working as it should. If you can take your crypto out of one wallet and put it into another wallet, you are all set!

Next Steps

Next, you can try using crypto to buy things in the real world and can consider accepting crypto as payment. Here are two recommended websites to help you begin using your crypto tangibly:

Buying: **www.usebitcoins.info**

This website provides an extensive directory of organizations that accept Bitcoin and other crypto tokens as payment. Art, toys, landscaping… if you want it, usebitcoins.info can help find places to use crypto to buy it.

Earning: **www.bitpay.com**

If you offer a product or service, you can use bitpay.com to start accepting crypto payments from your customers. bitpay.com offers a full checkout solution that can be installed on a website, allowing the user to accept Bitcoin and (if desired) convert it into fiat money.

* * *

You now know how to send and receive crypto! In addition to these, crypto can also be held as savings. The next chapter shows how to keep track of a crypto portfolio and explains why the price of crypto moves up and down.

Understand The Price

Anyone who acquires crypto will naturally become more interested in monitoring the price of it. The two best websites to view up-to-date crypto prices are:

- **www.coinmarketcap.com**, which has a simple, user-friendly interface. The default homepage shows the various crypto tokens ranked by **market capitalization** (i.e. the current fiat money price-per-token, multiplied by the total number of circulating tokens). The prices on the screen remain static until the page is refreshed, making them easier to view.

- **www.cryptocompare.com**, which is a more dynamic source. Here, the prices flash red and green as trades go through on the various online crypto exchanges. The site also gives a measure of the total US dollar volume traded over the last 24 hours, showing visitors which crypto tokens are experiencing the heaviest trading.

What Determines The Price?

The prices of crypto tokens are driven by the same two basic forces that influence all asset values - supply and demand. The market prices of US dollars, euros, and other fiat currencies are determined through the international foreign exchange markets. The values of crypto tokens are similarly decided through trading activity on the online crypto exchanges.

But why is there demand for crypto in the first place?

Admittedly, trying to put a valuation on crypto tokens is problematic. There are few of the traditional markers that investors normally use to value assets. Equity valuation relies on figures like revenue growth, price-to-earnings ratio, and dividend yield. Fiat currencies have the economic data of the country they represent - GDP growth, employment rate, trade surplus, and so on. Commodities like oil have production numbers and consumption rates. Many crypto tokens have no such anchor points. Therefore, we must consider other factors.

Scarcity

The supply schedule of Bitcoin is very limited - the software protocol ensures that only 21 million Bitcoins will ever be issued. Many other crypto tokens have similarly limited issuance schedules. Unlike fiat currency, there cannot be an infinite amount created, which is a big advantage for these crypto tokens vs. fiat currency. No central authority can arbitrarily decide to create more Bitcoin and thus devalue the savings of existing holders.

Scarcity is indeed an important property of crypto, but it is not the full story. Scarcity alone isn't enough to make something valuable. To be valuable, it must also have special utility.

Special Utility

Gold is a valuable metal because gold is <u>not only</u> rare, but is <u>also</u> universally considered exceptionally beautiful. Additionally, gold has useful physical properties - it is highly durable and is an excellent conductor of heat and electricity. Gold can be melted down and re-formed but never loses its luster. Together, these characteristics help explain why gold has been prized for thousands of years as a signifier of wealth, power, and prestige.

But what is the special utility of crypto? What can we do with crypto that we cannot do with anything else?

For all of gold's advantages, physical gold ingots are not practical at facilitating payments, especially over long distances. Gold is difficult to divide and transport. Gold is useful as a store of value, but it is far from ideal as a means of payment.

The special utility of crypto is that it combines some of the best features of rare, valuable commodities like gold (very limited issuance, privacy) with the best aspects of fiat money (highly divisible and digitally transmittable).

Bitcoin's anonymous founder, Satoshi Nakamoto, was fond of comparing Bitcoin to a physical commodity. This excerpt from one of his forum posts in August 2010 is insightful:[17]

"As a thought experiment, imagine there was a base metal as scarce as gold but with the following properties:
- boring grey in colour
- not a good conductor of electricity

- not particularly strong, but not ductile or easily malleable either
- not useful for any practical or ornamental purpose
- and one special, magical property: <u>can be transported over a communication channel</u>."[18]

Another special utility of crypto is **censorship resistance**. That is, central authorities cannot prevent the free movement of crypto. This is another aspect that makes crypto unlike government-issued money. Banks and governments retain the power to restrict and seize fiat money held in bank accounts - not so with crypto. Crypto can facilitate digital, international value transfers for those who need a censorship-resistant way to do so. Crypto is especially valuable for those who don't have access to the banking system, or who want their transactions to remain hidden.

Community Size

The intrinsic value of an individual crypto token is also influenced by the community that surrounds it. Michael Henman is co-founder of Invest In Blockchain, which oversees some of the fastest-growing websites in crypto. His view on crypto valuation places a heavy focus on community: "One of the most important and overlooked factors is estimating the potential network size, as well as the likelihood that this growth will be realized in the future. This can help predict the potential demand - and therefore future price action. For example, look at Bitcoin: every new store that accepts Bitcoin makes Bitcoin more useful, which attracts more users. You can apply this logic to most crypto tokens and then try to estimate how many people or businesses could actually use a crypto for a service or product."

If Bitcoin were a company, investors would say Bitcoin has built a "highly defensible market position". The effort that has gone in to the creation of Bitcoin and the other major crypto tokens cannot be easily copied. Bitcoin has traction, brand-name recognition, and a large number of developers, miners, applications, and users built up around it. As a crypto token gains community, it should become more valuable.

* * *

The next chapters turn to more advanced crypto topics. A working knowledge of these subjects will help you gain a fuller awareness of the bigger picture.

Forks

A crypto **fork** describes the situation in which a crypto token splits into separate branches, like the prongs of a dinner fork. This chapter looks at how forks occur, and why.

A Divergence In The Computer Code

Fiat money is decreed as the sole currency of legal tender within the country that issued it. By contrast, anyone who thinks they can make a better crypto token is free to start their own. This helps explain why there are well over 1,000 crypto tokens, compared to fewer than 200 government-issued currencies.

Crypto is computer code. Like any computer code, the code behind a crypto token can be written from scratch or copied from an existing set. When a crypto fork takes place, the original computer code is copied, modified, and given a new name. The result is a new crypto token.

When dealing with open-source computer code, copying is straightforward. The hard part for a new crypto token is getting other people to care about the new creation - to start using it, dedicate mining power to it, and form a community around it. While anyone could copy the open-source code of Bitcoin, the new tokens will be worthless if no one else recognizes them. Remember from the previous chapter that community is one of the primary drivers of the strength and value of a crypto token.

Several well-known crypto tokens had their start by forking from the original Bitcoin. In 2017, Bitcoin Cash and Bitcoin Gold both forked from Bitcoin. Litecoin was an even earlier fork, taking place back in 2011.

It may be helpful for readers to think of crypto forks as akin to a religious schism. In 1527, King Henry VIII became frustrated that his wife, Catherine of Aragon, had been unable to produce a male heir to the English throne. Henry wanted to marry another woman, but divorcing Catherine required permission from the Pope in Rome. When the Pope denied King Henry's request for a divorce, Henry decided to leave Catherine anyway. The Pope then excommunicated Henry, so Henry split England from the Catholic

Church and founded Anglicanism. Catholicism and Anglicanism share a common history, but since the 16th century, these two branches of Christianity have continued separately. Observers can still see what is shared between them - for instance, Catholicism and Anglicanism both feature the cross and study the Bible. But the divergence has resulted in important differences as well.

Why Do Crypto Forks Occur?

Like a religious schism, crypto forks feature differences of opinion that result in a split in the community.

One of the best examples is Bitcoin's debate around increasing the **block size limit.** The Bitcoin protocol limits the amount of data (and therefore, transactions) within each 10-minute block to 1 megabyte. From the book *The Age of Cryptocurrency*: "… the bitcoin network can currently process only about seven transactions per second, pitifully short of Visa's ten thousand." Some members of the Bitcoin community saw this 1-megabyte limit as a barrier to Bitcoin's future potential.

From a programming standpoint, it is trivial to increase the block size limit, but not everyone in the Bitcoin community thinks that this is the right thing to do. Opponents say the downsides of increasing the block size limit outweigh the benefits. They propose different solutions or believe that a low number of transactions per second isn't a problem at all because of their different vision for Bitcoin.

Trade-offs must often be made in software. Among Bitcoin's large, diverse community, it is not surprising that many different opinions abound. The path ultimately chosen will never be to everyone's liking.

After years of argument, on the 1st of August 2017, part of the Bitcoin community broke off and started a new token called "Bitcoin Cash". The new Bitcoin Cash community immediately raised the block size limit to 8 megabytes. The proponents of increasing the block size finally had their wish, but they had to leave behind the original Bitcoin community in order to get it.

What Happens When A Crypto Forks?

Anyone can copy an open-source project's computer code and introduce changes. This is what happens in a crypto fork. Both the original rules and the new rules have the same history at the point that the fork occurs, and the new rules only start to apply to the new blocks of the new, forked token. The below diagram illustrates what happens at the point of the fork.

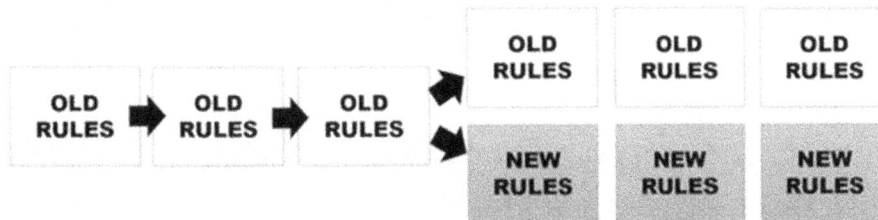

The extent to which the community is divided determines the strength of each network once the fork is over. If barely anyone leaves the original crypto token, then the new (forked) token won't gain much traction, and the impact on the original could merely be trivial. If, however, lots of users and miners leave and join the new crypto, it could significantly weaken the original.

What To Do If A Fork Is Coming Up

Here is what holders need to know if a fork is about to occur in a crypto that they own:

1. Tokens Are Safe

If Bitcoin goes through a fork, anyone who owned Bitcoin before the fork will still own all of that Bitcoin after the fork is complete.

2. Entitlement To The New (Forked) Tokens

A person holding 10 Bitcoin at the time of the Bitcoin Cash fork should also have received 10 Bitcoin Cash, while keeping their 10 Bitcoin. (Although there is an important caveat if the tokens are held in an exchange wallet - see below).

3. Exchanges May Not Distribute The Forked Tokens

Forks are a pain for online crypto exchanges. Their clients want the new crypto they are entitled to, but not every exchange prioritizes setting up new wallets and distributing the new tokens. When a fork is imminent, investors should make sure to hold their tokens in a wallet where they control their own private key.

4. Forks Usually Introduce Uncertainty

Uncertainty can scare off investors. Expect more volatility in the lead-up and immediate aftermath of a fork. Splitting off part of the community could weaken the original crypto if the split is large. Some investors prefer to sell before the fork and wait to see how the community sways.

5. <u>Note Which Block The Fork Is Scheduled To Occur</u>

Bitcoin Cash ("BCH") forked from the original Bitcoin blockchain after block 478,558 - the last common block before the split. From block 478,559 and later, Bitcoin and BCH were two separate tokens. For a holder to have received BCH, they must have held Bitcoin on the last pre-split block.

For the sake of clarity:
- Holders of 1 Bitcoin at block 478,558 would be entitled to 1 Bitcoin <u>and</u> 1 BCH after the fork.
- Selling after the fork does <u>not</u> affect their rights to BCH. They could sell their 1 Bitcoin the next block (478,559) and still keep the 1 BCH they received.
- Anyone who buys Bitcoin <u>after</u> the fork has taken place (block 478,559 or later) is not entitled to any BCH.

6. <u>The Original Token Price Should Drop Post-Fork</u>

Before the fork, the original crypto token comes with rights to the new forked token, whereas after the fork, those rights are gone. Therefore, some kind of drop in price is to be expected. It is similar to when a company on the stock exchange goes ex-dividend - once the dividend date passes, the price of the stock should theoretically drop to reflect the fact that dividends have been distributed.

* * *

The next chapter rounds out our education of crypto terminology with a topic which is both highly controversial and growing extremely quickly.

Initial Coin Offerings

The name "initial coin offering" was derived from the much older term "initial <u>public</u> offering" ("IPO"). An IPO is when a company lists shares of equity on a public stock exchange for the first time.

In 2012, Facebook conducted a US$16 billion IPO on the NASDAQ exchange. Once completed, ordinary members of the public could buy a slice of ownership in Facebook. Before the IPO, investors could only gain a stake in Facebook by negotiating directly with the company or with its existing shareholders.

Because of the strict rules imposed by securities regulators, conducting an IPO is a very expensive business. An IPO necessitates filing a prospectus - a long, prescribed document which details the company's investment case. To comply with regulations, the prospectus requires a great deal of input from lawyers and investment bankers, plus significant attention from the company's senior management. This cost and scrutiny makes conducting an IPO a landmark in a company's development. By the time Facebook conducted its IPO in 2012, it already had hundreds of millions of active daily users.

Options For Early-Stage Companies

But what about earlier-stage projects unable to bear the prohibitive cost of an IPO? If they can justify raising only a smaller amount - say, a few hundred thousand or a few million dollars - then it is not possible to afford all those expensive lawyers and bankers needed for an IPO.

With the IPO route too costly, the only realistic option for start-ups was to try and gain investment from angel investors or venture capital. When Facebook was taking its first steps, the Silicon Valley billionaire Peter Thiel was able to invest US$500,000 into Facebook in 2004 - roughly eight years before the IPO, and at a much lower valuation. The general public were legally prohibited from early-stage investing of this sort, as it was deemed "too risky" by regulators. But in the last few years, there have been two important changes to the landscape.

The advent of equity crowdfunding is one such change, which I wrote about in my first book: *Equity Crowdfunding: The Complete Guide For Startups And Growing Companies*. Equity crowdfunding saw regulators relax their laws to permit early-stage companies to raise small amounts of capital directly from the public under a reduced disclosure regime. Equity crowdfunding is like a mini IPO and is a lot less expensive to conduct. With equity crowdfunding, the company raising funds still needs to follow the rules, but the rules are far less burdensome.

The second innovation is the subject of this chapter: the **initial coin offering** ("ICO"). ICOs represent a fundamentally different philosophy to equity crowdfunding. Whereas equity crowdfunding sees issuers adhere to a simplified set of rules, ICOs use the features of crypto to exist mostly outside of regulation.

ICOs Do Not Use Fiat Money

ICOs ask investors to fund a project using crypto rather than fiat money. Because fiat money is not involved, ICOs are much harder to regulate.

Instead of investing fiat money in exchange for shares of equity (as in an initial public offering or equity crowdfunding), ICOs see one type of crypto (typically Bitcoin or Ethereum) sent by investors to the ICO project's wallet address, in exchange for the new tokens issued by the ICO project. At no point in the ICO process are banks or legally-defined securities involved - it's just one type of crypto being traded for another.

Regulators have tried to reign in ICOs by demanding that ICO issuers adhere to similar rules as traditional securities offerings, but crypto is borderless by nature. ICO projects can simply set up themselves wherever regulations are lightest. It is very difficult for regulators to prevent or restrict investors from sending crypto to ICO project wallets, regardless of where in the world the ICO project or the investors happen to be.

ICOs are not entirely immune from regulation, as Aziz Zainuddin, Founder of Master The Crypto explains: "One of the prominent traits of blockchain is transparency, where all transactions in the blockchain can be verified by anyone; you can look within a transaction and access all the details relating to it, from the sender's / receiver's wallet address, the exact amount transacted and the exact timestamp. It isn't private or anonymous, unless the sender /

receiver masks their wallet address. However, tokens that have an embedded privacy function may obfuscate identities linked to a wallet address. These tokens are much harder to regulate."

It must be emphasized that ICO investing is <u>extremely</u> speculative. It is an even higher-risk proposition than buying the better-known crypto tokens like Bitcoin (which are already quite volatile). If that bothers you, then ICO investing is not for you - and that's okay. Participating in ICOs isn't necessary to use most other parts of crypto. It is wise to build up hands-on experience with crypto basics before venturing into the Wild West of ICOs (if at all).

What Investors Need To Know

The surge of interest in ICOs has led to some dubious projects. Because there is little stopping anybody from starting an ICO, those in charge can run them however they like.

A number of projects will fail. These failures will include tokens which honestly try but do not succeed (after all, most start-ups fail, whether funded by an ICO or not). People will also start deliberate scams designed to enrich the founders at the expense of the investing public.

There was also the quite humorous "Useless Ethereum Token" ICO, which was completely up-front about the fact that the founder was going to run off with the investor's money. The token's logo was a raised fist giving the middle finger. The website plainly said: "You're literally giving your money to someone on the Internet and getting completely useless tokens in return."[19] This ICO still raised the equivalent of US$190,000 from those who were (presumably) amused enough by the audacity that they contributed anyway.

All joking aside, there is money to be made from ICOs too, which is why they continue to interest investors. Ethereum itself began as an ICO, and at the time this book went to print, anyone who participated in the Ethereum ICO would be very happy with how their investment has performed.

While ICOs are undeniably risky, "risk" is not exclusively negative. Risk carries the possibility of gain as well as loss. Some ICOs have returned 1,000 times their initial investment. When Peter Thiel invested in Facebook back in 2004, it too was a risky, largely unproven company - but that risk ended up paying off handsomely, and Thiel turned that US$500,000 into an eye-watering fortune of untold millions. ICOs allow members of the public to make their own highly speculative investments.

The key is to avoid foolish risks. At an absolute minimum, the proposal needs to have a solid idea, a plan, and a team with decent potential to make it happen. The document laying out the ICO project's ambitions is called the **white paper**. A white paper should contain information about the history of the project, the founders and other key people involved, a market overview, competitive analysis, and so on - ostensibly, everything a would-be investor needs to make a well-informed decision. A white paper is a bit like an IPO prospectus, but shorter and less legalistic.

Before doing any in-depth analysis about an ICO project, the first question an investor must ask is: <u>am I allowed to participate?</u> Some ICOs blacklist investors from certain countries.

For example, the Monaco Visa ICO excluded American citizens. An article on **www.bitcoin.com** explains why:[20] "American financial policies have circled the world through tax and compliance treaties that are enforced to varying degrees by signatory nations. Americans are required to disclose income earned and wealth held abroad to the IRS… And so, Monaco Visa asked every applicant a question: Are you a citizen of the United States? Those who checked the 'yes' box were directed to a page that stated, 'Sorry, your citizenship excludes you from participation in this ICO due to excessive regulatory risk from your SEC'."

What follows is a high-level overview of what else to look for in an ICO project. Again, remember that ICOs are a speculative investment with a high risk of potential loss. Buyer beware.

White Paper Analysis #1: Fundamental

Studying the inherent quality of the project is called **fundamental analysis**. Equity analysts perform a similar task during an initial public offering. Fundamental analysis involves evaluating what a project is worth and then comparing this to the offered share price, thus deciding whether it is undervalued or overvalued.

In the classic fundamental analysis book, <u>*One Up On Wall Street*</u>, Peter Lynch advocates for people to invest in what they understand. When it comes to ICOs, this means reading the white paper and getting to grips with the project before putting capital at risk. Below are some factors to consider in the course of fundamental analysis.

1. Is The Project Novel & Useful?

Just as a company needs to sell something that customers actually want, an ICO project needs to solve a real problem if it is to remain valuable in the long term. Before investing, make sure that the market will support what the project is proposing. Are competing projects already doing something similar? Even if not, could someone else easily copy this project's solution? Unique tokens which build something very hard to replicate will do best.

2. Existing Traction

How far along the path has the project already come? If all they have is an idea and a white paper, it isn't a good sign. Ideas are extremely common - what matters is the ability to execute. Ideally, the project should have been able to get some of the way towards realization before asking for funds from outside investors.

3. Team

Information about the management and key developers is essential to know. By reading the team bios, investors can get a sense of the backgrounds of those involved.

Ask: What is their prior track record? Ideally, this will not be their first foray into crypto tokens. Have members of the team conducted successful ICOs and built successful businesses in the past? Strong existing experience comes in especially useful when facing the inevitable roadblocks that come with any early-stage project.

Ravinder Deol of B21 Block Podcast says that ICO investors should follow the most talented developers. "What projects are these developers working on, what excites them the most? This is a good marker to filter out the pointless projects. Rather than assign the tangible assets as many would do with a traditional investment, look at the intangibles with ICOs. Are they strong enough?"

4. Professional & Easy To Contact

These days it is straightforward to create a professional-looking website, but some ICO projects still manage to screw this up. If they can't get their online presence right, it is a very bad sign. Are they active on social media? Are there typos and formatting errors in their white paper?

Investors may get more confidence in the people behind an ICO if they can physically meet them, shake their hand, and ask them questions in person. At the very least, there should be an easy way to contact them, and they ought to be responsive to questions. Investors can immediately disqualify ICOs if contact information is vague or nonexistent.

5. Relative Valuation

Valuing ICOs is admittedly fraught with difficulty. In many cases, there are no users, no revenue, no blockchain, and no intellectual property to base a valuation on. Still, one way to arrive at some form of valuation figure is by looking at past successful ICOs. If companies in a similar industry and at a similar stage of development valued themselves at less than US$5 million, but the ICO under analysis is at US$50 million, it is a red flag.

6. Who Are The Other Investors?

If an ICO is attractive, it will gain the attention and backing of well-known investors. This is important information to seek out. Having existing reputable investors commit to the project is strong validation for an ICO. If the ICO hasn't been able to convince any "smart money" investors to support the project, there is probably a very good reason why they have stayed away.

Participating alongside successful crypto investors allows others to effectively copy their strategy and follow in their footsteps.

7. Pathway To Project Realization

Look at what the project wants to do with the money they raise. The project should have a detailed budget laid out and a clear pathway to milestones they want to achieve. Again, it is about understanding the goal behind the project: is this ICO being conducted in order to develop something that doesn't exist yet, or is it about growing the marketing for an existing solution which already has demonstrable demand? The earlier that a project is, the more speculative it is.

White Paper Analysis #2: Deal Terms

This category of analysis is all about the structure of the deal rather than the project itself. It recognizes the fact that even a terrific project can still be a poor investment if the tokens involved are unattractive (and vice versa).

1. What Do Investors Get For Their Capital?

Instead of shares of equity, ICO projects may offer a share of revenue to token holders, a share of profit, a share of the underlying asset value that the tokens represent, or something else entirely. ICOs are less standardized than initial public offerings. Investors should make sure they understand the detail of what they are actually getting for their money.

2. Entry Point

As explained in *Cryptoassets* by Chris Burniske and Jack Tatar, "ICOs have a fixed start date and end date, and often there is a bonus structure involved with investing earlier. For instance, investing at an early stage may get an investor 10 to 20 percent more of a cryptoasset."

Early investors drive momentum in an ICO, which is why these investors are rewarded with a lower valuation when they buy in. A lower valuation is preferable because it implies more tokens for the same amount of invested capital. It is similar to the way that a cheaper "early bird" rate often applies to event tickets to encourage early sign-ups. Investors should know whether they are getting the best possible terms for their capital.

3. Funding Minimum & Funding Maximum

An ICO should set a minimum threshold, which if not reached will result in the ICO failing and all investors getting their funds returned. This is a critical feature because a project needs a certain amount of funding to do what they say they are planning to do. If they cannot raise this minimum, then they cannot attempt the plans that formed the basis for the investment.

The project should also have a funding maximum in place. ICOs without a funding maximum are signaling that they will take all the funds they are offered, which could cripple post-ICO demand for the tokens. ICOs with 2 times the demand for tokens compared to the number of tokens actually available can expect to have good price performance post-ICO because some of the investors who missed out on the ICO may try and fill their demand by buying after the ICO is over. But if the ICO project will issue all the tokens there is demand for, it removes this wall of unsatisfied demand and all the positive price tension that goes with it.

4. Founder & Key Person Token Allocation

It is suspicious if the founders allocate themselves too many of the new tokens. When Satoshi Nakamoto first launched Bitcoin, he didn't give himself a huge payload of Bitcoin to reward himself for having invented it. Every Bitcoin that Nakamoto ever received was mined, the same as everyone else's was.

Most ICO founders are not as altruistic as Nakamoto. People who work hard to create a valuable project want to profit from it, but it's a matter of degree. Picolo Research says that 10% of tokens to management is a reasonable benchmark for the amount of tokens held as a bonus for launching and commercializing an ICO project. The same report says, "In the event that you see the token allocation to management of 15%, you should flag this and ask why such a high proportion is kept by management."[21]

5. Founder & Key Person Lock-Up Period

ICO investors should make sure that the founders and key people have skin in the game. That is, they cannot exit from the project as soon as the ICO is over, sell their newly valuable tokens, and sail off into the sunset - leaving the ICO investors holding the bag.

The normal mechanism to ensure founders and key people have a strong reason to stay involved and drive long-term project value is to have their tokens subject to a **lock-up period**. Jose Mota is the host of Daily Crypto Podcast. His view is: "We have definitely been seeing an emerging trend of locking up tokens to incentivize not just founders, but also team members', users', and investors' tokens to combat turnover after an ICO is complete."

A lock-up period means founders and key people will not be able to sell their tokens for a certain period post-ICO. Commonly, their tokens will be unlocked on a set schedule - for instance, one third after 12 months, one third after 24 months, and one third after 36 months.

6. Investor Lock-Up Period

Equity crowdfunding investing and venture capital investing usually require years of waiting before shares can be sold. But ICO investors can often achieve an "exit" soon after the tokens begin trading on an exchange. This way, investors can cash out and recycle their capital into new ICOs, if they so desire. However, some ICOs restrict this by locking up investor tokens. Such restrictions make an ICO less attractive to invest in, all else equal.

7. <u>Scaling Mechanism</u>

Most ICOs work on a first-come, first-served basis to encourage people to invest as quickly as possible. But the more desirable ICOs can afford to scale using a maximum allocation policy - as in, they won't allow any single investor to get more than a set amount of the tokens.

Maximum allocation ICOs should end up with the tokens held by more investors, rather than concentrated in the hands of fewer large investors. It is a strong signal for an ICO to run their offer this way - albeit a risky one if the kind of widespread demand they were expecting fails to materialize.

Summary

Investors should make sure they take an approach in line with their risk tolerance. Great opportunities can go hand-in-hand with great risk - but investors must decide for themselves whether those are risks worth taking. By applying rigorous screening analysis to ICOs, investors should be able to protect themselves against becoming involved in the worst projects.

Is Crypto Just A Tool For Crime?

Once the features of crypto became apparent - particularly the strong anonymity - it didn't take long for lawbreakers to take notice. This has resulted in an unfortunate reputation for crypto.

Whenever the issue of regulating crypto is debated, the pro-regulation camp inevitably cites crime as a key reason for imposing strict rules, or for even trying to ban crypto altogether. *It finances terrorism! It facilities money laundering!* These are the sorts of arguments that can be hard to argue with, because to disagree seems to side with the bad guys.

But it would be wrong to throw away crypto just because criminals may use it. Instead, we should find ways of preventing the crime so that we can continue to use the desirable elements of crypto. This chapter examines the issues with crime and crypto.

Ransomware Attacks

Ransomware is a type of malicious software that either steals data or disables functionality from a computer or website. Then, the program demands payment from the rightful owner in order to return things back to normal.

Demanding this bounty through a bank wire is too problematic for a ransomware hacker - the payment can be easily tracked to the destination bank and even reversed. Cash isn't ideal for the hackers either - it opens the hacker to the strong risk of capture, as police could be stationed at the drop-off point. Crypto seems the perfect solution to facilitate a ransomware crime, as it is both digital and hard to trace.

But the problem of ransomware can be combated in ways other than regulating or banning crypto, such as through having more secure servers and more powerful passwords. Crypto only enters into the equation if the hack succeeds.

Silk Road

The most brazen case of crypto-enabled criminality was centered around a website called Silk Road. This online marketplace allowed users to buy and sell drugs, counterfeit documents, and other contraband. The full story of Silk Road is told in _American Kingpin_ by Nick Bilton.

Silk Road sellers would offer their wares for sale, priced in Bitcoin. Over time, sellers would develop a feedback reputation for high-quality goods and fast delivery, with a user interface resembling an online marketplace website.

Much to the chagrin of law enforcement, Silk Road was able to openly operate for several years. But eventually, the FBI was able to piece together the identity of the mastermind behind it all - Ross Ulbricht - and arrest him. The Silk Road website was replaced with a seizure notice from the Department of Justice. Observers quickly declared "the end of Bitcoin" (not for the first time or the last time). They assumed that with Silk Road gone, one of the main reasons that people used Bitcoin was gone too.

But interestingly, when Silk Road was shut down, the price of Bitcoin only dropped briefly. The price fell from US$140 down to US$110 within two hours of the news coming through, but the price was more or less back to where it had started just a few days later. The shutdown of Silk Road actually powerfully demonstrated that crime wasn't the only reason people were buying Bitcoin.

Some big investors even saw the dip as a fantastic chance to cheaply buy more Bitcoin. Quoting from _Digital Gold_, another book which covered the Silk Road saga in some detail: "… the Winklevoss twins saw an opportunity. The best analysis they had seen suggested that Silk Road accounted for no more than 4 percent of all Bitcoin transactions, hardly a driving force. More important, they knew that Silk Road was one of the biggest black marks holding Bitcoin back with ordinary people, who assumed the blockchain was just a payment network for drug dealers. This arrest could help sever Bitcoin's association with crime."

The fact that the FBI was eventually able to take down Silk Road also serves as a cautionary tale to criminals who think that crypto can provide them with a perfect shield against detection. Identities can be discovered, with enough effort, through the usual methods of detective work.

Marieke Flament, the Managing Director of Circle, points out that crypto transfers are often much more traceable than cash transactions: "Blockchain is a shared immutable ledger which records the history of transactions so it's actually better than cash for tracking where the assets have been and where they are going."

Cash is far more anonymous and used far more frequently in the drug trade than Bitcoin. The quantity of drugs bought and sold through Silk Road is absolutely dwarfed by the amount facilitated with plain old US$100 bills - yet no one is calling for US$100 bills to be banned.

It is true that illegal items were bought and sold through Silk Road. But as Andreas Antonopoulos said in *The Internet of Money*: "Throughout history, the most amazing technology is adopted by criminals first… The first cars were used as getaway vehicles. The first telephones were used to plot conspiracy. The first telegrams were used to run long-distance mail fraud schemes and Ponzi schemes. The first forms of electricity were used to run medical hoaxes and scam people."

Which brings us to the most salient point when it comes to crypto criminality…

The Good Comes With The Bad

Just because a tool can be used for nefarious purposes doesn't make it inherently bad. Knives can be used to slice bread or slit people's throats. Social media can be used to share vacation photos or recruit members for ISIS. Similarly, crypto can provide access to finance for the unbanked or transfer value internationally to rogue nations. Technology is agnostic to use.

As Harsh Agrawal of CoinSutra says, "Like gold or US dollars or any other fiat currency, crypto will always have use cases which don't fall on the right side of legality. But isn't that how money works? How can anyone ensure 100% that money will not be used for anything outside the law?"

So yes, criminals will use crypto, but crime is far more of an unfortunate side effect than a foundational feature. And like cars, electricity, and the Internet itself - the fact that crypto will be used by criminals does not mean that crypto is just a tool for crime.

Is The Electricity Used Wasteful?

A frequent criticism of crypto is the amount of electricity consumed by proof-of-work mining. All those industrial-scale server farms are <u>extremely</u> power-hungry. As of the end of 2017, Digiconomist estimated that the Bitcoin network was on track to consume 36.7 terawatt hours per year.[22] To put that in context, that's more than the annual electricity consumption of the Republic of Ireland, at 27.0 terawatt hours.[23]

We may conceptually acknowledge that scarcity is necessary to create value among crypto tokens, but it still seems wasteful. In a world already short of energy and facing real environmental challenges, it is reasonable to ask whether getting computers to churn through billions upon billions of hashes in competition with each other is a judicious use of precious electricity.

Further, the energy consumed by crypto is on an upward trajectory - in January 2018, Christine Lagarde, the head of the International Monetary Fund, warned that Bitcoin mining could soon consume as much electricity as Argentina, a nation of over 40 million inhabitants.[24]

An Arms Race

Proof-of-work crypto mining is an arms race. Arms races also occur in the military, in which two or more enemies compete to enlarge their armed forces. Each power spends more and more to try to outgun their foes, but the escalation often only results in the rivals canceling each other out.

All those resources used on building weapons could be spent on more socially desirable uses (like building schools and hospitals), but any power which opts out of the arms race runs the risk of becoming overwhelmed if their enemies continue building their arsenals. And so the arms race continues unabated.

The only way to stop an arms race is to get all the participants to come to an agreement to stop at the same time. Further, it must include some mechanism to punish cheaters. For example, many democracies cap the amount that politicians can spend on their election campaigns. These limits are legally enforced to stop campaign spending from getting out of control.

In crypto, such limits would take the form of miners collectively agreeing to slow themselves down. Roughly, if miners were to put in 10% of the work, then they would consume only 10% of the power. Unfortunately, the features of a crypto such as Bitcoin, together with human nature, make it unworkable to control the crypto arms race.

It is feasible to tell two rival politicians to limit their campaign spending and impose a penalty if they aren't true to their word. It is possible to sign a treaty to stop two rival powers from increasing their armaments and impose consequences if they break their promise, but it's impossible to get thousands upon thousands of independent crypto miners to limit their own profit when they are located all over the world.

Since crypto mining is inherently borderless and decentralized, a slowdown cannot be enforced. Each individual miner wants to run their machine as fast as possible. Even if some environmentally-conscious miners agreed to slow themselves down, other miners would surely choose to take advantage, cheat, and profit - and there would be no way to punish them.

Usage Occurs Where It Is Most Efficient

The first rebuttal to the charge that crypto uses too much energy is to realize that the energy used by crypto is occurring in places where there is already an oversupply of energy. Because crypto mining is agnostic to geography, miners gravitate to wherever electricity is cheapest and most efficient. Crypto isn't taking energy away from places where it is scarcest because it would be too expensive to mine there.

Instead, the electricity is largely coming from places like Iceland. Iceland's plentiful, inexpensive geothermal power is highly attractive for crypto miners, especially when combined with Iceland's naturally chilly climate, which helps keep the mining processors from overheating without as much need for artificial cooling.

Energy Is Used, Not Wasted

The second and more important point is that it is a mistake to characterize the electricity spent on crypto mining as "waste". It is more accurate to describe electricity as being <u>used</u> to replace swathes of incredibly resource-hungry trusted third parties.

Email servers also use a lot of electricity, but to only look at what those servers <u>consume</u> is to consider an incomplete picture. One must also consider the energy used by what email servers have largely replaced - namely, the postal service, with its mail trucks and postage stamps. Email has also sped up international communication by an order of magnitude, vastly improving productivity.

The resources saved through crypto are much more difficult to calculate than the energy expended in crypto mining. Anything that is hard to measure is frequently ignored - it's not legible if we can't quantify it. But resources saved through crypto are nonetheless very real.

As Paul Vigna and Michael J. Casey's _The Age of Cryptocurrency_ said, "… when we consider that world economic output runs to $87 trillion a year, and think of how much of that is hived off by the same banks and financial toll-collectors… it's possible to imagine many trillions of dollars in savings."

The best commentary on the matter was penned by Nick Szabo, a computer engineer who invented Bit Gold, which is a key predecessor to Bitcoin. In an article titled _Money, blockchains and social scalability_,[25] Szabo acknowledges that Bitcoin is not computationally efficient - moreover, proof-of-work is "intentionally very expensive". But because it helps solve the problem of trust, this inefficient machine can give us a more efficient human society.

Quoting from the article: "Bitcoin offends the sensibilities of resource-conscious and performance-measure-maximizing engineers and businessmen alike. Instead, the secret to Bitcoin's success is that its prolific resource consumption and poor computational scalability is buying something even more valuable: social scalability. When we can secure the most important functionality of a financial network by computer science rather than by the traditional accountants, regulators, investigators, police and lawyers, we go from a system that is manual, local and of inconsistent security to one that is automated, global and much more secure."

In summary, though it is undeniable that crypto consumes substantial energy, <u>it is worth it</u>, and likely saving more than it costs - although it is impossible to calculate precisely. Crypto helps people from disparate corners of the world to participate in the financial system and trust each other, without needing to rely on expensive third parties. We can't easily put a value on that.

Crypto frees people from the tyranny of local bureaucracies and laws, replacing it with a better system, using highly secure computer code. To achieve that, it is well worth dedicating a great deal of computer power and energy.

Hopefully, in time, the energy usage can also be reduced. As Matthew Aaron of the Crypto 101 Podcast predicts: "Bitcoin and proof of work will become more efficient in time just as the light bulb, automobile fuel economy, solar, or any other technology did as it evolved. If it does not, and the market finds a better solution to offer the advantages of proof of work without the energy consumption, then we will see a shift in use."

Is Crypto A Speculative Bubble?

Critics are fond of saying that "crypto is nothing more than a speculative bubble". What do they mean by this?

- **Speculation** is buying an asset in the hope of turning a quick profit, usually by betting on the price increasing. Speculators may not know anything about the asset they are buying (and indeed may not even care). The speculator merely wants to sell what they have bought to somebody else, later, for a higher price.

- **Bubbles** form when widespread speculation forces prices to spiral upward. New buyers enter the market to get in on the action - which creates even more demand, sending the price even higher, in a self-reinforcing feedback loop. So long as people keep buying, the price keeps rising, thus confirming to speculators that they should buy even more.

History tells us that bubbles tend to end unhappily. Eventually, prices painfully crash back down as the speculators try to sell their holdings *en masse* as quickly as possible. In the aftermath, everyone swears that the madness will never happen again - until the next speculative frenzy takes hold and all is forgotten.

In late 2017 / early 2018, crypto prices experienced a sharp fall. Bitcoin nearly touched US$20,000 per unit, but within a few months had plummeted to well below US$10,000 per unit (more than halving, in US dollar terms). This seems to confirm to crypto skeptics that the tremendous price rises of 2017 were characteristic of a speculative bubble.

Are they right? It is tough to say because one of the defining characteristics of speculative bubbles is they can only be confirmed as such with the benefit of considerable hindsight. You will only be able to place the 2017 / 2018 crash in its proper historical context if you are reading these words several years in the future - was it a blip, or did crypto prices stay depressed for a long time?

Speculation Can Happen To Any Asset

If the history of financial markets has taught us anything, it is this: <u>any asset</u> can become a bubble if speculators believe there is the potential to make a profit from it.

Here is a (partial) list of some of the assets that speculators have influenced over the centuries:
- Stocks
- Bonds
- Options
- Currencies
- Real estate
- Gold (and other commodities)
- Fine art
- Mortgage-backed securities
- Credit default swaps
- … and crypto.

Speculation is nothing new - bubbles have occurred in financial markets for centuries before crypto existed. If people are speculating on crypto, they are just doing the same thing as they have always done: gambling on the future in the hope of making a quick gain. Speculation will continue to be a fact of life for real estate, stocks, and fine art too - but no one is calling for an end to building houses, creating companies, or painting pictures.

It isn't possible to ban crypto - but even if it were, it wouldn't be possible to ban speculation or bubbles. Because of human nature, bubbles will continue to occur forever.

Fast-Rising Prices Could Be Justified

Just because prices have risen very quickly doesn't <u>necessarily</u> mean that a speculative bubble exists. Burniske and Tatar's book *Cryptoassets* points out that a crypto token's market price includes both **speculative value** and **utility value**, and it is difficult to disentangle the two.

If crypto represents the architecture upon which we can replace large swathes of trusted third parties, then the utility value may have caused the explosive price growth. It is possible for prices to <u>justifiably</u> rise rapidly.

Let us look at the stock price of the Internet retailing giant Amazon.com as a case study. In the late 1990's, Amazon stock was bid up to what were (at the time) astronomical levels. Back then, Amazon had never made a profit, yet investors were still buying like crazy. It had all the hallmarks of a bubble.

Then, in the early 2000's, the dot-com bust struck, and pessimism took over. The new narrative became that Amazon would soon get crushed by the incumbent brick-and-mortar retailers like Borders and Walmart as they started their own online offerings.

The below chart shows how Amazon's stock price moved between its initial public offering in 1997 through to 2002 (the nadir of the dot-com bust).[26]

But here is the important point: we need to look at this 5-year episode in its proper historical context. Next, let's look at Amazon's stock price performance through from 1997 to mid-2018 - a bit over 20 years. The same 5-year period between 1997 and 2002 is visible on the far left but barely registers because of what Amazon's stock price has done subsequently.

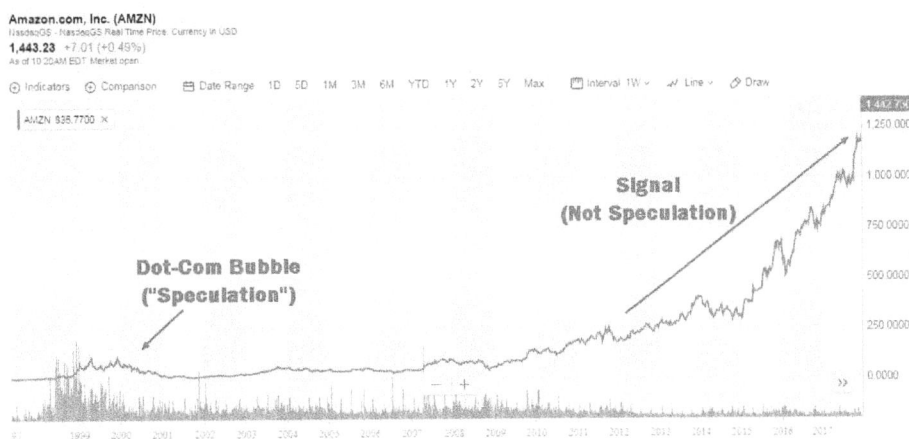

Amazon's story imparts an important lesson: don't pay attention to the **noise**, pay attention to the **signal**.
- Noise = Short-term ups and downs.

- Signal = The long-term big picture.

As we now know, in Amazon's case, the "signal" was that the Seattle-based online retailer was on the path to global domination. Amazon has become one of the most valuable companies on the planet, firmly ensconced as the world's preeminent online shopping destination. Amazon's stock price today cannot be called a "bubble". Instead, it is at these levels due to a change in the company's intrinsic utility value. The lesson is: <u>in the long run, the signal dominates the noise</u>.

What does this mean for crypto? Although crypto speculation will inevitably continue, in the end, speculation is just noise compared to the true story: decentralization, permissionless transactions, and access for all. That is what will eventually matter for crypto value.

The Price Is Not Everything

While investors and the media gravitate towards tracking the price, it needs to be emphasized that the short-term price of a crypto and its intrinsic utility value are <u>not the same thing</u>. Be cautious about reading too much into the price. Just because prices may have recently got ahead of themselves (or crashed) shouldn't count as a strike against the technology.

Unfortunately, most people don't understand this sort of nuanced view, especially when it is so easy to instead fixate on a single number, like the price. When prices collapse, the media pronounces that crypto is dead, when it is more likely to be a case of speculative value disappearing. Always consider the possibility that the intrinsic utility value may not have changed - it might just mean that the speculators have fled. The dot-com bust of the early 2000's didn't represent the end of the Internet - far from it. The Internet is still around and stronger than ever.

HODL

As you continue to learn about crypto, you might hear the following: "**HODL**". The crypto community disagrees whether "HODL" is a typo when "HOLD" was intended, or an acronym standing for "Hold On for Dear Life". Whatever the case, it means: don't sell at the worst possible moment (when everyone else is selling).

This is a critical mantra for readers who truly believe in the long-term future of crypto. Do not get seduced by short-term price movements. Ride the ups and downs. People who have been in crypto for years have seen it all before - the collapse of the Mt. Gox exchange, the arrest of the ringleader of the Silk Road marketplace, interventions by governments… all events that were supposed to spell the end for crypto, and yet crypto still endures.

Where does all this leave us? There are three key takeaways:

1. There are no set rules in financial markets. Sometimes asset price rises are bubbles that pop, and sometimes asset price rises can be justified, because they represent a genuine change in the state of the world (like in the case of Amazon).

2. Asset prices comprise both utility value <u>and</u> speculative value. It is impossible to exactly know how much of each makes up a price, but remember that a rise or fall in price could be due to either reason. Focus on the signal, not the noise.

3. Over the long term, asset value should tend towards utility value. So look for crypto tokens which have usefulness, community, and a defensible position. Don't be too concerned by the short-term cycles of boom and bust.

One thing is for sure: the future of crypto will include speculation, bubbles, and a crash here and there. We can't expect speculators to stop being greedy - we just have to learn to live in a world where they are always going to exist.

On a more tactical level, Zach DeWitt of the Token Talks Podcast has some sound advice for spotting a speculative bubble as it is forming: "I think a clear sign that we are in a speculative run-up is when crypto seems to dominate your social conversations. In December 2017, I remember being in a workout class and seeing the person next to me check the Coinbase app three times! This was certainly a signal that the markets were in a mini bubble."

While the effects of crypto speculation will continue to dominate the news-cycle-obsessed media, in the grand scheme of things, what is far more critical is the strength of crypto and blockchain as technologies. And therein will be the <u>real</u> story of crypto over the coming years.

What Will Governments & Banks Do?

Crypto is now firmly on the radar of bank executives and government officials. These institutions are not going to sit idly by and just wait for disruption to happen to them.

When considering the possible response of governments and banks, remember that "governments" and "banks" do not think with a single hive mind. Different governments and different banks are bound to come up with widely divergent answers to the questions posed by crypto. Banks are engaged in open competition for revenue and customers. Similarly, governments are competing for taxes and citizens.

To be sure, some governments will try to squeeze the life out of crypto through regulation. For instance, in September 2017, China made it illegal for Chinese start-ups to raise funds through initial coin offerings.[27] Although the decentralized nature of crypto makes it impossible to completely shut down (short of turning off the entire Internet), governments can still make life harder for crypto.

But crypto innovation will always find a home where regulation is more favorable. To stamp out Bitcoin would require deleting every copy of its blockchain, everywhere in the world. If Bitcoin can survive anywhere, it survives everywhere. Some governments seem to understand this. In December 2017, the Baltic nation of Estonia proposed to launch the "Estcoin"[28] - a state-sanctioned crypto token designed to attract initial coin offering activity to Estonia's shores - quite a contrast to China! It shows that at least some forward-thinking governments are viewing crypto as an opportunity to gain a competitive advantage over other countries rather than as an existential threat to their existence.

Similarly, while some banks will demand regulation to protect the status quo, others have shown interest in trying to integrate aspects of crypto for themselves. Banks are currently exploring using blockchain technology as a replacement for the convoluted existing system of payment processors and clearinghouses to verify international transactions. This could drive down fees and clearing times.

However, there are bound to be critical drawbacks to any government / bank crypto tokens. Governments and banks are unlikely to offer the privacy features of open-source crypto. It is hard to imagine a government / bank blockchain without mandating that names, addresses, and other identifying information are attached to the wallets. Very likely, they would also retain the right to deny accounts, monitor the transactions, and freeze accounts deemed to be making "unacceptable" transactions. If so, government / bank blockchains would reintroduce many of the most critical drawbacks that come with trusted third parties.

It also seems highly improbable that government / bank blockchains would allow private individuals to set up mining rigs to plug into their proof-of-work pool. Without this, government / bank crypto will not be as secure as the larger open-source proof-of-work crypto tokens (such as Bitcoin), with their security strengthened by self-interested miners. Remember, the amount of computer power dedicated to hashing is one of the key methods for securing the blockchain from attack. No single government server can provide anything close to the power of the larger open-source crypto networks.

Even so, there will be users who prefer a government / bank crypto token - either because they don't understand the drawbacks, or because they don't care about them. Those who find open-source crypto confusing and opaque might prefer to trust a government / bank crypto instead of Bitcoin purely because of better brand-name recognition. At least governments and banks are "the devil they know".

But even if governments and banks start their own crypto, the exciting thing is that <u>a choice will exist</u>. People will no longer <u>need</u> to use the government / bank system of value transfer if they don't want to. History has shown that whenever monopoly power is eroded, it results in lower prices and better service for end users.

Ultimately, if governments and banks want to compete with open-source crypto tokens, then they will need to make their offering attractive. Instead of having exclusive power to issue currency, governments will need to compete in the free market. If a government / bank crypto retains too many of the flaws that motivated people to build crypto in the first place, then they will find themselves swept away by competition.

Watch this space.

Conclusion

What is the future of crypto? That is the multi-trillion-dollar question. Will crypto and blockchain technology completely replace the need for fiat currency and trusted third parties? Is crypto just a passing fad, soon to be forgotten as a footnote of history? Or (more likely) will the reality lie somewhere in between?

It is worth keeping in mind that just because an innovation is new doesn't necessarily make it an improvement over what came before. And even if it is a better way of doing things, a new technology can still struggle to gain mainstream adoption. Steve Jobs once breathlessly predicted that the Segway (the two-wheeled self-balancing scooter) would be as big a deal as the personal computer![29] That prophesy turned out to be very wide of the mark - today, Segways are mostly used for tourist novelty rides. Even the biggest crypto optimists should bear this in mind as a cautionary tale. What matters isn't that crypto is new - instead, what matters is what crypto can do, and whether a critical mass of people will prove willing to use it.

It is impossible to know what the future holds, but crypto has a lot of people very excited. By any measure, it is impressive how far crypto has come in a relatively short space of time. In under ten years, crypto has gone from an unknown project on an obscure cryptography mailing list to arguably the hottest topic in finance and tech.

Despite the inherent uncertainty, this concluding chapter provides some perspective on the possible future of crypto, including the obstacles it needs to deal with and a few predictions to look out for.

Challenges That Crypto Must Overcome

1. Highly Volatile Price

Individual crypto tokens routinely rise or fall by 10% in a day (when measured in fiat money terms). Yuval Gov of CryptoPotato argues: "In order to have more widespread crypto adoption, crypto must become a lot more stable. Extreme volatility, like we see in most of the cryptos, prevents usage of them as a store of value."

Dealing with exchange rate volatility is something that anyone who earns in one currency and spends in another has to contend with. For instance, a person who earns primarily in euros but spends primarily in US dollars experiences similar purchasing power fluctuations due to movements of the USD / EUR exchange rate, which is beyond their control.

Even so, it must be acknowledged that crypto volatility is particularly severe and needs to settle down if it is to gain more widespread acceptance. This might well be the biggest thing holding crypto back. Many people are understandably nervous about accepting crypto as payment because they fear the gyrations in value - even if it could change for the better. When it comes to money, most people tend to be highly risk-averse. They prefer to know that the value of their savings isn't going to change too much.

A workable crypto economy needs to develop for the volatility problem to diminish, and this will take time. Currently, those who accept crypto as payment still base their crypto prices on the day's fiat-crypto exchange rate. But as the crypto ecosystem matures, sellers must become more willing to charge purely in crypto, rather than tethering it to the value of crypto vs. fiat. That way, people can become more confident that their crypto earnings today will still be able to buy the same goods and services tomorrow.

2. Not Widely Accepted

Crypto suffers from a chicken-and-egg problem: people are wary of accepting crypto as payment because they are worried they will struggle to find others who will accept crypto when they want to spend it.

This is not an insurmountable obstacle. Countless other technologies have overcome the chicken-and-egg problem in the past. Just think - the very first telephone was useless, as there were no other telephones for it to call. Only once a second person had a telephone did telephones become useful. The second telephone gave the first telephone more utility. The telephone got even better once a third person joined - the experience for the first two telephones improved because of the addition of the third telephone and so on, into eventually millions and billions of telephones.

This well-known phenomenon of a technology becoming more useful with each additional user is known as a **network effect**. We have recently seen network effects kick in with email, social media, and online shopping. All had to begin from a standing start. Crypto needs to gain broader acceptance, but just because it is hard to find people willing to accept crypto today doesn't necessarily mean it will always remain that way.

3. Ambiguous Legal Status

Lawmakers, regulators, and courts are starkly divided about how to classify crypto. Crypto arrived into a world with existing laws which never imagined it, and these laws still haven't caught up.

The US Internal Revenue Service classified Bitcoin as property.[30] Meanwhile, Ecuador declared crypto illegal.[31] And the Hong Kong Monetary Authority labeled it a commodity outside of its jurisdiction to regulate.[32]

Some may argue that since crypto is decentralized and borderless, the law doesn't matter to crypto. But legal ambiguity discourages mainstream adoption. The world urgently needs lawmakers who properly understand how crypto works and are willing to create a coherent framework that works with it rather than tries to fight it.

Predictions For Crypto

1. In The Long Term, Prices Will Trend Upward

Crypto tokens like Bitcoin are inherently **deflationary**. Because the supply of Bitcoin is constrained, existing units should increase in value over time if adoption increases. This is a great feature for those who hold their crypto as savings. It's similar to the reason why many investors favor real estate as a store of value. As the American writer Mark Twain once said: "Buy land. They're not making any more."

Unlike fiat money, whose supply has absolutely no ceiling (meaning the value of each unit declines as more is brought into existence), there will only ever be a fixed number of Bitcoin produced. If Mark Twain were alive today, he might have said: *Buy Bitcoin. They're not making any more than 21 million of them.*

Will there be bumps along the way as bubbles of speculation pop into troughs of despair? Most certainly. Will some individual crypto tokens turn out to be duds? Definitely.

But if we zoom out and take a 10,000-foot view of the big picture of crypto:

in the long term, value will move based on how compelling the technology is. _The Crypto Intro_ has argued that crypto has a bright future, but you need to make up your own mind. Just remember - pay attention to the long-term signal, not the speculative noise.

2. User-Friendliness Will Continue To Improve

Using crypto still isn't intuitive enough. Think of the slick design of a modern smartphone - even a young child can quickly figure it out without needing to read the instructions. In fact, many smartphones don't even come with instruction manuals anymore - smartphones are so easy to use that instructions aren't required. By contrast, crypto doesn't work too well out of the box. This complexity deters people.

Let's recall what the early days of email looked like. The modem necessary to connect to email was hard to buy and even harder to install. Then, the modem took over the phone line when it was turned on. It was expensive, with access paid by the minute. And very few other people had email addresses anyway - so even if a user got online, it wasn't possible to reach most of their contacts via email.

Most people who looked at email in those early days would have laughed at the idea that it would someday put mailmen out of work. As Ofir Beigel of 99bitcoins put it, "You have to remember we're just in the beginning of the crypto revolution. Email was invented in 1972, yet it took over 20 years until people started using it."

The same is true of any new technology. Early cellphones were the size of bricks. Early cars were slower than horses. Crypto still has some growing up to do, but many clever and well-resourced companies are working on coming up with solutions. Over time, we can expect to see better and better ways of making crypto more intuitive to use than today.

3. A Consolidation In Crypto Tokens

There has been an explosion in the number of so-called **altcoins**, many of which introduce no new innovation. They might alter the supply schedule or tinker with the mining algorithm - but many of them are mere copycats, nothing more than an existing token with a different logo.

Earlier, this book explained that the intrinsic value of a particular crypto asset is driven in large part by the community it builds. In the view of this author, there aren't enough users to sustain so many different altcoins. I predict a shakeout similar to the early days of the Internet. Remember AltaVista, Ask Jeeves, and AlltheWeb? Eventually, all became insignificant compared to Google, because Google does the best job of being a search engine. Expect to see crypto communities cluster around the best-in-class tokens, and the others to quietly fade away.

Parting Thoughts

If you want to see the future, follow the money. Venture capital can see the opportunity in crypto, and the people in charge of making their investment decisions are jumping in with both feet, committing hundreds of millions of dollars.

To visualize how popular crypto already is, visit **www.bitlisten.com**. This website represents Bitcoin transactions with circles of small or large size, accompanied by a sound of high or low pitch, depending on the value transacted. It quite stunningly demonstrates the extent of existing Bitcoin use. Seeing and hearing Bitcoin is far more powerful than arguments and statistics.

But the most powerful way to learn crypto is to try it for yourself. If you are ready to take action, the next section offers step-by-step guidance for how to do that.

Acknowledgments

My sincere gratitude goes to these outstanding organizations that contributed to *The Crypto Intro*:

- B21 Block Podcast
- Master The Crypto
- Invest In Blockchain
- Coinsutra
- Crypto 101 Podcast
- SatoshiLabs
- CryptoPotato
- 99 Bitcoins
- Daily Crypto Podcast
- Circle
- Coinmama
- CryptoCompare
- KeepKey
- Javvy
- Token Talks Podcast

Thank you for adding your most valuable insights!

Glossary

Altcoins: "Alternative Coins" - a crypto token which is not one of the largest and best-known ones like Bitcoin, Ethereum, or Litecoin.

ASIC: "Application-Specific Integrated Circuit". A specialized piece of mining hardware specifically designed to do the mining task for a certain hash algorithm. Tend to be faster but less flexible than GPUs.

Asymmetric Key Cryptography: A way of securely encrypting and decrypting data using paired cryptographic keys. The public key is used to encrypt data, and the private key is used to decrypt data.

Bid-Ask Spread: The difference between the best price proposed by buyers and the best price offered by sellers.

Block: A set of transactions which are grouped together by a miner and permanently recorded on the blockchain.

Block Reward: The newly-issued crypto awarded to the successful crypto miner every time they are able to add a new block to the blockchain. This provides an incentive to crypto miners to dedicate computer power to the maintenance of the network.

Block Size Limit: The maximum amount of data which can be contained in a single block.

Blockchain: A form of digital ledger which chronologically records blocks of transactions, stretching all the way back to the start of the network.

Bubble: A situation where speculative buying causes an asset price to increase dramatically for reasons other than that asset's utility value.

Censorship Resistance: The ability for a transaction to be executed without any third party preventing it. It is one of the main characteristics that makes crypto valuable.

Cold Wallet: A crypto wallet without access to the Internet. Less accessible, but more secure than hot wallets.

Crypto: Digital assets which are secured by cryptography.

Cryptocurrency: A subset of crypto - tokens which are specifically designed to act as currency (e.g. Bitcoin).

Cryptography: A branch of computer science which deals with privacy and encoding.

Deflationary: Describes an asset which should increase in value over time due to limited issuance characteristics.

Digital Currency: Any currency represented digitally by data, rather than physically, like banknotes. Cryptocurrency is a digital currency, and government-issued money can also be a digital currency (e.g. credit card payments and international bank wires).

Distributed Ledger: A decentralized record of value ownership. In crypto, instead of a single party being the designated recordkeeper (as with a bank), many different parties share this responsibility.

Fiat Money: Government-issued currency decreed as the currency of legal tender within the borders of the country that issued it.

Fork: The situation where a crypto token splits into separate branches. Both tokens have a shared history but will evolve separately after the fork is over.

Fundamental Analysis: Evaluating the value of a project with regard to its underlying utility value rather than speculative value.

Gatekeeper: A person or group that can control and potentially deny access.

GPU: "Graphics Processing Unit". Used for crypto mining, they tend to be slower than ASICs, but can be flexible across multiple hashing algorithms.

HODL: A slang term within the crypto community meaning to "keep hold of crypto instead of selling it".

Hardware Wallet: A cold wallet storage option which stores the user's private keys in a secure hardware device.

Hashing: The process of turning data into an encoded output. Used in proof-of-work crypto mining. It is a one-way process - it is possible to take data and turn it into a hash, but not possible to take the hash and find out the original data.

Hexadecimal: The base-16 numbering system used in Bitcoin hashing.

Hot Wallet: A crypto wallet with access to the Internet. More accessible, less secure than cold wallets.

Immutable: A record which cannot be changed after it has been created.

Initial Coin Offering (ICO): An offering of new crypto tokens for the first time. Involves a white paper to outline the purpose for the project.

Key: Cryptographic keys effectively "store" crypto on the blockchain and enable the owner to access and spend it. Keys come in pairs - a public key and a private key.

Limit Order: An order to trade if certain criteria are met - for example to sell crypto if a minimum price is reached.

Liquidity: Volume of trading activity in a marketplace.

Lock-Up Period: In ICOs - prevents founders, key people, and / or investors from selling their tokens for a certain period post-ICO.

Market Capitalization: The current price per crypto token multiplied by the total number of circulating tokens outstanding. Gives a measure of the market value of the network.

Market Order: An order to execute a trade immediately, using the best price proposed by other existing market participants.

Maximum Threshold Number: As crypto miners find hashed outputs, they test their outputs against this network-generated "threshold" number. If their output is smaller than the threshold, the miner gets to create a block and collect the block reward.

Middleman: A party which stands in between a buyer and a seller, often collecting a fee along the way.

Mining: Dedicating computing power to helping maintain the network. Involves playing a competitive game of chance against other miners to be the one to update the blockchain.

Network Effect: The positive effect that each additional user brings to existing users by making the network more useful through them joining.

Noise: Short-term price movements often driven by speculators. (Opposite to "signal".)

Nonce: An arbitrary number added to the transactions by miners to try and create a different hash output.

Online Crypto Exchange: Websites that allow users to buy and sell crypto with other traders.

Private Key: The half of the cryptographic key pair required to send payments. It must be carefully protected, as anyone who has access to the private key also has access to all the crypto associated with it.

Public Key: The half of the cryptographic key pair required to receive payments. It can be disseminated widely, with no risk.

QR Code: A representation of data (in crypto, typically a wallet address) through a square barcode. Scanning a QR code replaces the need to enter the data manually.

Round-Trip Cost: The total cost of trading in and out of an asset, inclusive of exchange fees and crossing the bid-ask spread.

Scarcity: Rareness. This is one of the essential characteristics for an asset to have monetary value.

SHA-256: The hashing algorithm used in Bitcoin's proof-of-work system.

Signal: Long-term value movements driven by a change in the state of the world, such as greater adoption / traction. (Opposite to "noise".)

Speculation: Trading in an asset in the hope of a quick gain.

Speculative Value: The part of the crypto price which is driven by speculators and expectation of what the token's price may become in the future.

Token: An individual crypto asset. Bitcoin is one, Ethereum is another, Litecoin is yet another.

Trusted Third Party: An entity which facilitates interactions between two parties, whom they both trust.

Two-Factor Authentication (2FA): An extra layer of security which requires that a smartphone app generate a one-time code to be entered by users before performing certain functions with exchanges and wallets.

Utility Value: The part of the crypto price which is driven by the token's intrinsic usefulness, community size, etc.

Wallet: A place which stores cryptographic keys to make them more legible to humans. Software wallets, paper wallets, and hardware wallets are some of the varieties.

White Paper: The business plan and technical manual behind a new crypto token. It lays out what the project plans to do, and how.

Zero-Sum Game: A competitive situation where one party's gain is another party's loss. Proof-of-work crypto mining is a zero-sum game because all miners are competing over a fixed quantity of new crypto issued.

Copyright & Disclaimer

1.   www.reuters.com/article/us-senate-virtualcurrency/virtual-currencies-vulnerable-to-money-laundering-u-s-justice-idUSBRE9AH0P120131118

2. As an aside, there really was an island that used stones similar to these for this purpose. The island is called Yap, located in the present-day nation of the Federated States of Micronesia. The rest of the story in this section has been made up and is not historical.

3. www.ted.com/talks/dilip_ratha_the_hidden_force_in_global_economics_sending_money_home

4. www.bitcoin.org/bitcoin.pdf

5. Those interested in learning more about government surveillance are strongly recommended to watch the award-winning documentary *Citizen Four*, which tells the story of Snowden and the revelations he uncovered.

6. www.ustream.tv/recorded/11319925

7. www.globalfindex.worldbank.org

8. www.news.gallup.com/poll/1597/confidence-institutions.aspx

9. "Trust" as measured by respondents who said they trusted the institution in question either a "Great deal" or "Quite a lot" on the 4-point response scale.

10.   www.medium.com/@cryptoeconomics/the-blockchain-economy-a-beginners-guide-to-institutional-cryptoeconomics-64bf2f2beec4

11. Not a real address

12. www.mtgox.com/img/pdf/20140228-announcement_eng.pdf

13.   www.news.com.au/finance/money/investing/dont-tell-my-wife-melbourne-man-cries-over-lost-bitcoins-as-price-surges-past-us10000/news-story/bd18b6f6aa123dca017f9cc75544fd01

14. This number, "50 million", has been made up - for illustrative purposes.

15. www.unenumerated.blogspot.com/2017/02/money-blockchains-and-social-scalability.html

16. www.support.coinbase.com/customer/portal/articles/2924446-irs-notification

17. www.satoshi.nakamotoinstitute.org/posts/bitcointalk/428

18. Emphasis added

19. www.uetoken.com

20. www.news.bitcoin.com/some-icos-now-ban-americans-who-should-expect-more-ostracism

21. www.picoloresearch.com/20/the-beginners-guide-to-investing-in-icos

22. www.digiconomist.net/bitcoin-energy-consumption

23. Source: International Energy Agency, at www.iea.org

24. www.bloomberg.com/news/articles/2018-01-25/lagarde-says-cryptocurrency-mining-is-consuming-too-much-power

25. www.unenumerated.blogspot.com/2017/02/money-blockchains-and-social-scalability.html

26. The prices shown on this graph have been adjusted for stock splits.

27. www.forbes.com/sites/kenrapoza/2017/10/18/chinas-blockchain-bitcoin-ban-no-match-for-stateless-cryptocurrency-market

28. www.medium.com/e-residency-blog/were-planning-to-launch-estcoin-and-that-s-only-the-start-310aba7f3790

29. www.content.time.com/time/business/article/0,8599,186660-1,00.html

30. www.irs.gov/newsroom/irs-virtual-currency-guidance

31. www.ibtimes.co.uk/ecuador-reveals-national-digital-currency-plans-following-bitcoin-ban-1463397

32. www.news.takungpao.com/paper/q/2013/1116/2042791.html